# STRONG *and* COURAGEOUS

## STUDYING GOD'S PROMISES IN JOSHUA

DONNA SNOW

CONCORDIA PUBLISHING HOUSE • SAINT LOUIS

Have I not commanded you?
Be strong and courageous.
Do not be frightened,

and do not be dismayed,
for the Lord your God
is with you wherever you go.

***(Joshua 1:9)***

# STRONG *and* COURAGEOUS

## STUDYING GOD'S PROMISES IN JOSHUA

DONNA SNOW

# Dedication

THIS BOOK IS WHOLLY DEDICATED TO JESUS CHRIST,
MY LORD AND SAVIOR, WHO CARRIED ME KICKING AND SCREAMING
THROUGH MY DESERT WILDERNESS OF UNBELIEF INTO HIS GLORIOUS LIGHT
OF FAITH ROOTED IN HIS PROMISED LAND.

Published by Concordia Publishing House
3558 S. Jefferson Ave., St. Louis, MO 63118-3968
1-800-325-3040 · cph.org



2 3 4 5 6 7 8 9 10 34 33 32 31 30 29 28 27 26 25

# WHAT PEOPLE ARE SAYING

Donna Snow did it again: this study on Joshua will open up the living Word of God for you, breathing God-given grace-life back into your weary and wandering heart. *Strong and Courageous* will strengthen you with God's Spirit of courage and boldness founded on His never-failing faithfulness. Soak in the Christ-centered lessons on leadership, trust, and the awesome work of God then and now for you!

**Rev. Michael W. Newman, president, LCMS Texas District; author of *Faith Notes: A Christ-Centered Survival Kit for Young Men***

Donna Snow's *Strong and Courageous* delves into the book of Joshua and points us to Jesus. Joshua . . . is a wonderful picture of a devoted servant of God and a faithful model of a godly leader. Covering this epic story with a mix of abundant historical research, thought-provoking applications, and personal stories, Donna challenges us with a rich study filled with Scripture. It's an in-depth study of God's judgment and wrath, along with His grace and mercy. I'm a huge fan of these tremendously well-done studies!

**Rev. Dr. Gregory Walton, president emeritus, LCMS Florida-Georgia District**

Donna again brings her unique insights to this exploration of God's Word, relating the message of Joshua to our world today. Her citations of other Scripture passages throughout this study show the unity of God's Word, and she seamlessly connects the message of Joshua to what Jesus did for us through His life, death, and resurrection.

**Rev. Michael Mattil, pastoral counselor, 2007–11, Lutheran Women's Missionary League; pastor emeritus, Grace Lutheran Church, Denison, Texas**

Embark on an inspiring journey through the book of Joshua with Donna Snow as your trusted guide! This engaging study dives deep into themes of faith, courage, and God's unwavering promises with thought-provoking insights, practical applications, and meaningful reflections. . . . Whether you're exploring the bold leadership of Joshua or the miraculous battles fought in faith, this study will equip you to face challenges with confidence and walk in greater obedience to God's Word.

**Rev. Vince Parks, executive pastor, Salem Lutheran Church, Tomball, Texas**

In Donna Snow's newest Bible study, God's truth and His promises shine through each page. Using Joshua's example, we, too, can win the battles we face each day because we know that our heavenly Father will never leave us or forsake us. I always appreciate Donna's dedication to God's Word. I'm honored to have been able to preview this amazing study. I guarantee you will love it as much as I did.

**Janetta Messmer, Christian author and beta reader, Edits by JM**

This insightful study on Joshua by Donna Snow shows us that Joshua had sun-stopping, giant-tromping, unstopping, enemy-whomping faith—the kind of faith believers need right now in this unpredictable world! Snow skillfully highlights Joshua's uncompromising faith that propelled him to be strong and courageous in the Lord despite harrowing situations. A God pleaser, not a people pleaser, Joshua remained stalwart because of God's promises to him. *Strong and Courageous: Studying God's Promises in Joshua* is an anthem for every believer as we face off with the giants in our lives.

**Linda Kozar, author, BroadStreet Publishing**

Donna Snow's study of Joshua is a Bible student's dream. Donna has yet again written high-quality, well-researched, thorough-yet-digestible content that focuses on God's presence and His promises. This eight-week study is infused with supporting Bible passages and engaging questions to help a reader dive deeply into God's Word. I can't decide which I like more: Donna's relevant connections from Joshua to real-life leadership and conflict situations or her "Go Quiet, Go Deep" at the end of each lesson. This study is a must-have!

**Rev. Jason Schleicher, spiritual formation pastor,**
**Salem Lutheran Church, Tomball, Texas**

As one who has walked through a significant leadership transition, I was struck again by Joshua's story of following Moses and leading the Israelites into the Promised Land. Donna's passion for reading, digesting, and harvesting applicable truths from Scripture comes through in spades in this study. Get ready to dive in, dive deep, and be reminded that we can wholeheartedly put our trust in God, who is our "wall-flattener, javelin-holder, and sun-stopper"!

**Rev. Tim Niekerk, senior pastor, Salem Lutheran Church, Tomball, Texas**

# Contents

# INTRODUCTION

The book of Joshua dramatically details one of the most significant changes in the history of God's people. After forty years of wandering in the wilderness, the time has finally arrived to enter and conquer the land God promised to Israel. At long last, wandering in circles is replaced with "Forward, march!" Can you imagine the Israelites' excitement and wonder at what they would encounter?

The book of Joshua opens in 1406 BC, after the death of Moses. The first and great leader of the Israelites is gone. He had led God's people while they were enslaved in Egypt, led them through the plagues, guided them through the Red Sea out of Egypt, and led them as they wandered in the desert for forty years. The profound sense of loss among the Israelites is palpable through their grief.

God has set the stage for the children of Israel to receive their promised inheritance at long last. God's people will finally steer their caravans into the land God had promised to Abraham more than six centuries earlier. Yet Moses, the only leader the Israelites had ever known, would not put even one toe onto the soil they were promised. Can you imagine the uncertainty or even fear that the Israelites likely experienced? Now, God raises up and commissions Joshua to take Moses' place as leader of His people. The Israelites knew Joshua as one of their own. Committed. Dedicated. Faithful. But Joshua is no Moses.

There is a significant amount of warfare in the book of Joshua. You may find it hard to understand that level of physical conflict. However, you and I can certainly understand conflict. These postpandemic years have been fraught with conflict in the United States. We also understand conflict in our families, communities, and even our churches. Although you might not be able to relate to physical combat, as you walk through this study of Joshua keep in mind the conflicts you have experienced these past few years. God's promises of salvation and redemption never fail.

It is difficult to understand or justify God's commands for Joshua and his soldiers to attack a town and leave nothing breathing. But together we will read God's Word and continually ask for discernment and wisdom. God's ways are not our ways. His thoughts are not our thoughts. We cannot fathom the mind of God.

We will look at the important parallels between the book of Joshua and the apostle Paul's letter to the Ephesians. Here in Joshua, God's people enter and possess an earthly inheritance promised to Abraham. Paul shows in Ephesians how the church entered and possessed a heavenly inheritance secured by Christ.

Many other theological themes are found in both Joshua and Ephesians, such as godly leadership, rest, holiness, and obedience. As the Israelites followed God in order to possess their promised inheritance, Christians today follow Christ so that we may possess our promised spiritual blessings on earth, anchoring our hearts in heaven.

So, as we embark on this study, I ask you to remember three specific things:

1. God is sovereign, His plan is perfect, and He keeps His promises.
2. God gave the Canaanites more than six hundred years of grace to turn to Him. To come to repentance. To see the Lord as their living God. Yet, they steadfastly followed the lifeless gods of this world.
3. We will never see the wrath of God to that degree because of Jesus' sacrifice on the cross.

We may not understand or relate to the bloody hand-to-hand combat that Joshua and the Israelites experienced. However, we can understand warfare on a different level. Warfare exists in global politics, power struggles, and financial domination. The warfare for our souls rages on the internet, in mass media, in the movies, and on television programs that point people to self instead of to Jesus.

We understand conflict. We feel it every day. We may not physically see it the way Joshua and the Israelites saw it; however, the devil prowls like a roaring lion looking for those to devour (1 Peter 5:8). Following God's commands as the Israelites did is crucial. Even when warfare gets bloody (as it does in Joshua), God keeps His promises.

It is thrilling to read about the miraculous collapse of Jericho's walls. To be struck with awe at our magnificent God who holds the sun and moon still in the sky. To share in the thrill of victory at the heart-stopping battles as the Israelites take possession of their God-given inheritance.

The book of Joshua is about stepping into the promises and the Promised Land of God. Rich spiritual treasure awaits us as we study familiar stories such as Rahab and the spies, the nightless battle when the sun appears to be still in the sky, and the walls of Jericho tumbling into rubble. This verse-by-verse study strives to awaken us to underlying theological truths, how they apply today, and what they reveal about our promise-keeping God.

My prayer is that this study brings the fullness of God's story to beautiful and glorious clarity for you. May this study strengthen your faith in our miracle-working, promise-keeping God.

# HELPFUL INSIGHTS INTO THE BOOK OF JOSHUA

Joshua, the first book in the Bible to bear the name of its author, can be summed up by one verse: "Not one word of all the good promises that the LORD had made to the house of Israel had failed; all came to pass" (Joshua 21:45). Under Joshua's incredible leadership, the people keep their eyes on the Lord and work together. The result is a turning point in the timeline of God's people as they see proof that God fulfills all His promises.

At its core, the book of Joshua shows how the Israelites received the inheritance God promised, which parallels our blessing of the new covenant under Christ.

The Pentateuch (the first five books of the Bible; also called the Books of the Law) focused on establishing God's Law and on laying the foundation of God's will being known. In Joshua, we see how the Israelites operate based on that foundation. Not a single law is contained in Joshua. The emphasis throughout the book is not on establishing commands but on illuminating the abundant blessings of faithful obedience to the Lord.

Joshua picks up immediately where Deuteronomy ends: at the death of Moses. Since leaving Egypt, not a single Israelite had known a spiritual leader other than Moses. Just think of Great Britain in our modern era. Queen Elizabeth II reigned for more than seven decades; much of the United Kingdom had never known another monarch. The Israelites were embarking on physical and spiritual new territory: life without their beloved leader Moses.

## The People, the Land, and the Promise

The book of Joshua provides the history of God's people settling into the land He promised to Abraham and his descendants (see Genesis 12:7; 22:17–18). Land is the central focus of the book, which is divided into three distinct sections: (1) entering the land, (2) conquering the land, and (3) dividing the land.

While the Pentateuch laid out God's Law, Joshua provides a fitting resolution and logical conclusion to the Pentateuch in that it shows the manifestation of God's faithfulness to keep His promises. Exodus shows the initial movement toward the land; Numbers continues the journey and discusses land inheritances. This first book after the Pentateuch showcases the fruit of obedience and the consequences of unbelief. Just as God fought for Joshua and the Israelites, He fights today for every believer against the schemes of the enemy.

Some scholars have suggested that the book of Joshua should be included with the Pentateuch under the name "Hexateuch" since some of the patriarchal promises had not yet been fulfilled. In fact, because Joshua is so intricately linked with the land promises of God in Genesis, the prophet Isaiah describes the coming Messiah as if He were a second Joshua who would "establish the land, . . . apportion the desolate heritages" (Isaiah 49:8). However, even though the uninterrupted timeline continues into Joshua, the life and leadership of Moses does not. Consequently, the Books of the Law logically remain as only the first five books of the Bible.

## Authorship and Date of Writing

Many books in the Bible are named for the author who wrote them. However, it is not clear that Joshua wrote all of this book. Some Bible scholars believe he wrote many significant parts because Joshua 24:26 tells us this: "And Joshua wrote these words in the Book of the Law of God." But some portions were likely completed by the Deuteronomistic writers (the writers after Moses who gave us the Books of History) around the seventh and sixth centuries BC or even as late as the time of King David. Some suggest that Joshua may have dictated portions to a scribe or that scribes simply compiled and edited manuscripts from Joshua's day. Most notably, Joshua's death is recorded, which Joshua would have been unable to write.

Scholars generally agree that the exodus happened around 1446 BC and date the writing by Joshua between 1406 and 1380, with some portions of the book added at later dates (such as those about Joshua's death). We could spend much time narrowing down more precise dates as scholarship and archaeological discoveries continue to emerge, but such is not the focus of this study. Rather, these dates provide a time frame from which to launch our adventure into the book of Joshua.

Joshua is the first book in the historical category of the biblical canon known as the Prophets. It is followed by Judges, 1 and 2 Samuel, and 1 and 2 Kings. Interestingly, the book of Joshua is included as a "book of prophecy" in the Jewish Torah. While the book of Joshua is historical in its events, it is also prophetic as it declares the reality of God and His work among us. Even though Joshua was known as a gifted military commander, he was a prophet like Moses. He heard from God and spoke for God. In fact, chapter 24 shows Joshua delivering a first-person message from God to His people.

When we view the book of Joshua as prophesy and the fulfilling of God's promises, it reminds us that God is the true hero of this book. This truth applies to every book in the Bible. Joshua was the faithful servant that God used to accomplish much.

I pray that this study will enrich your faith walk and understanding of God's beautiful plan of redemption for His people.

## Lesson 1

# THE COMMISSIONING OF JOSHUA

*(Joshua 1–2)*

At one of the most crucial times in the Israelites' history—the death of their leader—God indicates that He has provided His people with a new leader with one simple word: *after*. God chooses Joshua, Moses' assistant, to lead the throng into the Promised Land. God begins by encouraging Joshua three times to be strong and courageous, and He affirms that He will be with Joshua just as He was with Moses.

With God's presence among them (through the ark of the covenant), and with His promises ringing in his ears, Joshua steps up as the new leader of God's people to take them into the land promised to them through Abraham.

Day 1: Joshua's History and Early Years (Exodus and Numbers)

Day 2: Moses' Legacy and Death (Joshua 1:1–2)

Day 3: God Commissions Joshua (Joshua 1:3–9)

© Concordia Publishing House

Day 4 : Joshua Assumes Command (Joshua 1:10–18)

Day 5: Rahab Hides the Spies (Joshua 2)

**Key Questions:**

- What are the characteristics of a godly leader?
- If you have served in any kind of leadership role, what were your biggest challenges?
- When was the last time you were truly excited about stepping into a plan that God laid out before you? What happened?

## DAY 1

# JOSHUA'S HISTORY AND EARLY YEARS

*(Exodus and Numbers)*

When I encounter an impactful leader, I am curious about his or her backstory. There are usually life-transforming moments that God orchestrates and leverages to elevate that leader above the rest. There is always a story. So, let's look at Joshua's story.

Joshua first appears on the pages of Scripture in Exodus 17. Born as a slave, he is part of a nation laboring under the cruel whip and brutal hand of Egypt's pharaoh. Joshua has never breathed the clean air of freedom. By the time God sent Moses to liberate His people, the Israelites had been in bondage for a *very* long time. But all that was about to change dramatically.

Amid the desperate cries of His people trapped in captivity, God set in motion His plan to fulfill the promise He had made to Abram centuries earlier in Genesis.

**In Genesis 12:2, what did God promise?**

In the very next chapter of Genesis, Abram was standing in Canaan, the Promised Land. Over time, there is deceit and loss, drought and famine. Six hundred years later, as the book of Joshua opens, God's people have grown into a great nation, but they are enslaved in Egypt. Cruel oppression and heavy burdens occupy their days. So God called Moses to liberate His people at long last.

**According to Genesis 13:14–15, to whom did God make the promise?**

God's promise was not to just one man but to that man's offspring for all time. So, with Joshua faithfully at his side, Moses led the people out of Egypt and into the desert. As Moses led God's people through the wilderness, Moses' highest desire was to follow the Lord wholeheartedly.

**What did Moses say to the Lord in Exodus 33:15?**

What faith! Another way to say it could be "Don't give me the Promised Land without the Promise Keeper's presence." Perhaps it is wise to stop and ask ourselves if we want the good gifts God brings or if we want Him. Stuff or Savior? Comfort or the Christ? Moses wanted God's presence above all else. Joshua witnessed Moses' declaration (Exodus 33:11). What a powerful example of God-honoring leadership for Joshua to emulate during his leadership in the Promised Land.

Joshua appears numerous times in the Pentateuch. Read and note how Joshua appears in the following verses:

**Exodus 17:8–13**

**Exodus 24:12–13**

**Exodus 33:11**

**Numbers 11:26–30**

**When you read those verses, what stands out to you about Joshua?**

Joshua could always be found with Moses or where Moses commanded him to go. Whether dutifully serving by Moses' side or patiently waiting outside the tent of meeting, Joshua was faithful to God. His love for the Lord shined clearly through his devoted service to Moses. Joshua diligently put God first in his life.

**If you have observed or worked with such a leader, what did you learn?**

**What does Numbers 27:18–19 say about Joshua?**

Joshua is a man in whom the Spirit of God resides. And we can see the Spirit working in and directing Joshua's steps. You and I have the Spirit of God in us through the gift of Baptism.

**How is God directing your steps in this season of life?**

In Numbers 13–14, Moses sent spies into the Promised Land to see what awaited the Israelites. Out of the twelve spies, only Joshua and Caleb brought back positive reports. Joshua and Caleb emphatically state that the people should enter because the Lord had promised the land to them. However, Moses and the people chose fear over faith and did not enter Canaan. Their failure to trust God results in that entire generation (everyone except Joshua and Caleb) being sentenced to die in the desert without ever entering the Promised Land.

Faithfully following God—even in fearful, uncertain circumstances—is the hallmark of a believer's trust in God.

Take a moment to recall a time when you followed God past your fears. **How did that experience impact your spiritual journey?**

According to the following verses, what was the responsibility of Joshua, along with Eleazar the priest?

**Numbers 32:28–29**

**Numbers 34:16–17**

When God's people eventually settle in the land, God assigns to Joshua the gargantuan responsibility of properly distributing the lands among the tribes. God faithfully equips Joshua for his task just as He equips us for ours.

### Joshua's Name

Few details are provided regarding Joshua's family. According to the following verses, what do we know about Joshua and his family?

**1 Chronicles 7:20–29**

These verses only provide the name of Joshua's father, the tribe to which his family belonged, and the location where they lived. Joshua's tribe comprises the descendants of Ephraim, one of the two sons of Joseph born as he served in Egypt. However, Joshua's name was not always Joshua.

**In Numbers 13:8, what is Joshua's name?**

Joshua's original name, Hoshea, means "salvation" or "deliverance." So where did his new name come from?

**Write out the last sentence of Numbers 13:16.**

Moses gave Joshua his new name. The name *Joshua* or "Yehoshua" means "Yahweh saves" or "Yahweh delivers." That change is significant because it affirms that God alone is the one who saves and delivers His people. God Himself was Israel's deliverer and no one else. Joshua would lead them, but God was their Commander in Chief.

There is more. Joshua's new name is a form of how Jesus' name is said in Hebrew: Yeshua.

What do the following verses say about the name of Jesus?

**Matthew 1:21**

**Philippians 2:9–11**

God sent Jesus as our deliverer—through Christ's blood shed on the cross for us—and no one else. Foreshadowing the salvation of His people through the promised Messiah, God raised up this man named Joshua—Yehoshua—to deliver the Israelites into the Promised Land. Joshua's new name is a constant reminder to the Israelites that God is our faithful Promise Keeper.

Being assigned a new name was not unique to Joshua. God often changed the names of those who would do mighty works for Him through faith. For example, Abram, "exalted father," became Abraham, "father of many nations." Simon, "listen or hearing," became "Peter," the "rock."

As Christians called to faith in Jesus, we all have a new name: Redeemed. Thank You, Jesus, for that beautiful truth.

## GO QUIET, GO DEEP

Quiet your mind from distractions and pull your Bible close. Bow your head and ask Jesus to make His Word and today's text personal for you.

Take your time writing out Psalm 103:12.

What does it mean to you that God has removed your transgressions and does not hold them against you?

I pray that you walk in the freedom of God's redemption to shine His light into a dark world.

## Day 2

# MOSES' LEGACY AND DEATH

*(Joshua 1:1–2)*

The book of Joshua opens at a significant, transitional moment in Israel's history. Their great leader, "the servant of the Lord," has died. The only earthly leader God's people had ever known was gone. Imagine the questions and turmoil in their minds! But God already has a new leader picked out: a faithful, devoted servant of the Lord named Joshua.

**How is Joshua referred to in Joshua 1:1?**

Four times in Scripture, Joshua is referred to as Moses' aide, which simply means "one who serves." Joshua served Moses faithfully, and now he has some huge sandals to fill. However, no one could fill Moses' shoes, including Joshua. Moses was Israel's great lawgiver. He was the one God met with face to face. Through Moses, God had worked mighty miracles on behalf of the Israelites. It is not a stretch to assume the people might have been anxious about the leadership succession.

**If your church or business has faced any significant leadership transition—especially a pastor or CEO—what questions or fears did you have?**

**Did you discuss your fears with fellow parishioners or coworkers?**

**How has God worked through that situation to strengthen your faith?**

We can relate to the anxiety or questions that God's people may have wrestled through regarding who would succeed Moses. Just think back to your country's most recent selection of a leader. It is human nature to want to know the last chapter of the story before opening the book, so to speak. Anxiety can run high, but Christ-followers trust that all things rest in God's hands and perfect plan.

Moses is called "the servant of the LORD" more than a dozen times in Scripture. The majority of those times occur in the book of Joshua. Interestingly, Joshua is called "the servant of the LORD" only twice at a specific time in his leadership.

Read and write out those two verses:

**Joshua 24:29**

**Judges 2:8**

**Why do you believe Joshua is referred to as "the servant of the LORD" only at his death?**

Think of a funeral you have attended for a person who had accomplished much in his or her life. The list of achievements may be impressive in scope and breadth. However, more often than not, the person's most significant, far-reaching accomplishments did not happen until the later years of his or her life.

At Joshua's death, it is clear that he had followed God faithfully and fulfilled his God-given obligations as Israel's leader. After eighty years of faithful service, Moses was not allowed to bring the Israelites into their inheritance. I don't know about you, but after listening to whiners in the desert for forty years, Moses' denied access seems unfair to me. However, it is not a permanent denial. Moses is present at the transfiguration of Jesus, which occurs in the Promised Land. God's grace to Moses is a beautiful reminder of His grace to us even when we mess up.

**Read Numbers 20:6–12. What action prevents Moses from entering the Promised Land?**

God clearly instructs Moses to *speak* to the rock, not *strike* the rock.

**Why do you believe that nuance made a difference?**

Since Moses strikes the rock instead of speaking to it, some people could have argued that the force of Moses' two strikes instead of God's power could have shifted the rock to bring forth water.

**What does God say about His power in Isaiah 42:8?**

God is crystal clear in Scripture that He will share His glory with no one. Moses has failed to uphold the Lord as holy, so the Lord does not allow Moses to enter the Promised Land.

**Do you find it hard to follow God's Word when there seems to be a better way to do certain things? Why or why not?**

Regardless of our personal opinions, following God and His plan according to His Word is crucial. (God clearly instructed Moses to *speak* to the rock.) Not obeying God's commands casts us outside of His will for our lives. Moses was a sinner like you and me. And like us, Moses felt the consequences of disobedience.

Even so, Moses was a faith-filled man greatly used by God. It is nearly impossible to summarize the legacy of Moses in a single chapter, much less a single sentence. But one verse fits well.

**Write out John 1:17.**

The bottom line is that Moses embodied the Law. As crucial as that is, observance of the Law will never lead us to the fullness of God's promises and goodness. The grace and truth of Jesus, based on the promises given by God through Moses, will lead us into the promised land of eternity.

Read and write out the following verses that confirm that beautiful truth:

**Acts 15:11**

**2 Corinthians 8:9**

**2 Timothy 1:8–9**

The saving grace of Jesus Christ leads us home to the Father. Through God's inspiration, Moses laid out the Law that Jesus fulfills through His life, death, and resurrection. Moses taught the people God's Law, but Joshua leads them to God's promise.

Before Moses died, he requested from God a specific kind of leader to replace him.

**Read Numbers 27:16–20. What kind of leader did Moses request as his successor?**

Moses is concerned that the people would wander without a godly leader, so God puts his mind at ease and instructs Moses to choose Joshua as his successor. Moses had worked with Joshua for decades and knows that Joshua is a man of strong faith and integrity.

**From the verses above, what did God tell Moses about his successor?**

According to God's instructions, Moses laid his hands on Joshua and passed along his authority. The "laying on of hands" is found in Scripture in several different scenarios (as is anointing with oil). Here, it is a ceremonial blessing of authority.

In the New Testament, Jesus often lays His hands on people to bless and heal them:

Matthew 9:18

Mark 5:23

Mark 6:5

Mark 7:32–33

Mark 8:22–25

Luke 13:13

Jesus also lays His hands on the little children so they would come to Him and be blessed (Matthew 19:13–15; Mark 10:16).

**Have you experienced the "laying on of hands"? If so, how did you feel afterward?**

And as Moses neared the end of his life, he ensured that the people would remember Joshua as his successor and their leader.

At some point in our lives, we also need to choose successors, whether in business or family.

**What kind of person would you choose to succeed you and why?**

**Read Deuteronomy 31:7–8. What stands out to you in these verses?**

Moses not only said those words over Joshua—he said them in the presence of all Israel. Joshua is designated by God Himself, and blessed by Moses, to lead the Israelites into the Promised Land.

**What is the result of Moses' laying on of hands according to Deuteronomy 34:9?**

The people trust Joshua because he had been chosen and anointed by God. I would argue that the people also trust Joshua because he had been there all along. The people know Joshua. He has led war on their behalf, served Moses faithfully, and suffered in the desert right alongside them. He is one of them.

Think of those Christian brothers and sisters who hold a special place in your heart. Chances are you have been through hardships and heartaches together. You trust them with your home, your children, and even your life. They follow God wholeheartedly and inspire you to do likewise.

The Israelites follow Joshua because Joshua follows God. As we read through the incredible life story of Joshua, you will discover for yourself that Joshua was ALL IN right from the start.

## GO QUIET, GO DEEP

Quiet your mind from distractions and pull your Bible close. Bow your head and ask Jesus to make His Word and today's text personal for you.

Take your time writing out Numbers 6:24–26.

What does it mean to you to be blessed by the Lord for His service?

I pray that the Lord continues to bless you and give you peace as you faithfully serve Him with gladness.

## Day 3

# GOD COMMISSIONS JOSHUA

*(Joshua 1:3–9)*

As today's text begins, we discover that the narrative continues from Deuteronomy to Joshua almost seamlessly. Deuteronomy ends with Moses' death, and the book of Joshua picks up at Moses' death without interruption. God immediately calls Joshua to step forward and lead His people into the land He promised them through Abraham.

After wandering in the wilderness for forty years, the death of Israel's great law-giver signals a change in direction. God stops circling the wagons and points the people straight ahead to their long-awaited destination.

**Read Joshua 1:3–5. What stands out to you in these verses?**

Can you imagine the elation of Joshua and Caleb? Finally! Thirty-eight years after they had returned from their initial scouting mission and told the Israelites to trust God and enter the land, they are the only two adults from the Egyptian exodus that God preserved to cross over.

Joshua had road experience. He would not be leading the people blindly into the unknown. He and Caleb had seen for themselves what awaited God's people. First-hand experience is valuable.

Often it takes experienced Christians going before us to show what's possible when we trust God.

**Which people has God given to you in that capacity? How did their experience and trust in God help you?**

God encourages believers today by pointing us to the Old Testament roster of men and women who were used greatly by God despite monumental challenges and have served to strengthen our faith.

**What does Paul tell us in Romans 15:4?**

We can take heart! We can have hope! God uses His Word, past events, and godly leaders to strengthen our faith to forge ahead.

One of the things I most admire about Joshua is that he stood tall and led with God-given authority. He never shifted blame or made excuses. His unwavering devotion to the Lord fueled his leadership journey.

## Preparing Israel's New Leader

The time has come for God's people to enter the land of Canaan. But before they gather their belongings to cross the Jordan, much preparation is required.

For instance, they have to come to grips with the fact that the death of Moses would not hinder their forward momentum. God's faithfulness does not vanish in the face of funerals or rivers. God is faithful in every age, and He would be in this one as well. So, first and foremost, God prepared His chosen leader, Joshua.

If you have responded to God's call for a leadership role, you know it requires God-given devotion, strength, and courage. Effective leadership also requires hands-on experience, and God provided Joshua with extensive experience as Moses' right-hand man.

Only the Jordan River stands between the Israelites and their promised inheritance. The Israelites need to walk by faith and overcome significant obstacles to receive the promises of God.

**If you have served in any kind of leadership role (large or small), what were your biggest challenges?**

**What were your biggest blessings?**

**How did God show Himself faithful?**

There is a small but significant word from Joshua 1:2 that is repeated in verse 3: *give.* That one word reminds every generation that the task set before Joshua was really the work of God. The same is true for the tasks that God sets before us today.

### The Land

Joshua 1:3–5 outlines the land that God promised the Israelites. There are several similarities to the words used in Deuteronomy 11. Take a moment to write out each:

| JOSHUA | DEUTERONOMY |
| --- | --- |
| Joshua 1:3 | Deuteronomy 11:24a |
| Joshua 1:4 | Deuteronomy 11:24b |
| Joshua 1:5a | Deuteronomy 11:25a |

Repetition provides vital assurance that God is faithful to keep His promises. The same promises God gave to Moses would be granted to Joshua.

**In Joshua 1:3, what land does God promise to give His people?**

That is an exceptionally broad parameter! Everywhere they walk within the boundaries of the Promised Land will be given to them. We will see how much of it they actually walked on and claimed toward the end of this study (Hint: It was not all of the Promised Land).

As you saw from the exercise above, Joshua 1:4 contains a crude map that generally describes where the boundaries fall in the Promised Land. To the south lies the desert, to the north sits modern-day Lebanon (including two mountain ranges), on the eastern boundary runs the Euphrates River, and to the west lies the Mediterranean Sea. This is a broad picture taken with a wide-angle lens. We will zoom in on that picture throughout the course of our study.

## God's Promises to Joshua

**In Joshua 1:5, what incredible promise does God make to Joshua?**

This verse provides the spiritual highpoint and heart-warming promise of God to Joshua as Israel's new leader. God would give His people success. Most important, God would never leave Joshua. He even promises to be with Joshua in the same way that He was with Moses.

**Write out Deuteronomy 31:23.**

God's promise to Joshua never changed. In fact, the phrase "I will be with you" reminds us of identical promises God made to Isaac (Genesis 26:3), Jacob (Genesis 31:3), and Moses (Exodus 3:12). Then, God expands on His promise to Joshua that not only would He be with Joshua but He would never leave nor forsake Joshua.

As New Testament believers, we have that same promise through our Lord and Savior Jesus Christ. Write out the following verses:

**Matthew 28:20**

**Hebrews 13:5**

**How does this promise of God encourage you to remain steadfast in your faith today?**

God's presence with Moses was the key to his success. So it would be with Joshua. So it is today in the church. And so it is with every believer. God's presence is the power-packed secret to a successful, God-honoring life.

Along with God's promises to give, God continues His inaugural speech to Joshua to add encouragement and direction.

**Read Joshua 1:6–9. What particular command does God give Joshua three times?**

After God promises to remain with Joshua, God commands Joshua to "be strong and courageous."

Write out these three verses:

**Joshua 1:6**

**Joshua 1:7**

**Joshua 1:9**

**What similarities and differences do you notice between these verses?**

In physical terms, you may picture being strong and courageous as standing straight, throwing your shoulders back, and sticking out your chest. But that posture does not fit the context. God encourages Joshua to rely on Him just as Moses had.

Joshua could be confident because God is capable.

Joshua could rely on God because God is reliable.

Joshua could trust God because God is trustworthy.

For people in leadership roles, Joshua 1:9 is one of the most powerful verses in Scripture. God does not tell Joshua that he *might* face difficulty along the journey. Ministry and leadership are fraught with fear and discouragement. The only remedy is a constant awareness of God's faithful presence.

The Hebrew word for "be strong" (*hāzaq*) in Joshua 1:6–9 refers to being strong in the sense of personal strength. The Hebrew word for "be courageous" (*āmēts*) in those three verses conveys an imperative to be bold. Such strength and courage are found only in the Lord.

To lead God's people well, Joshua needs to both be strong and courageous in the Lord and trust the Lord's promise. After all, if a leader lacks either, then any cause he or she pursues would face grave peril. Joshua needs the Lord's strength and courage to be completely obedient to Mosaic Law.

It is vital to remember that even though Joshua leads, he is the guide, not the Giver. He is the director, not the Deliverer. God alone delivers His people into the Promised Land.

**When you face daunting situations, how do you remind yourself to be strong and courageous in the Lord?**

Think about it. Joshua and the Israelites had personally experienced dramatic visual confirmation from God. They witnessed miracles never seen before. And the scale of those miracles has never been seen since.

**What does Exodus 13:21–22 tell us?**

That vision of God leading them by day and night never leaves their memories. Joshua is also the first person to see the face of Moses glowing with God's radiance as he descends holding the stone tablets of God's Law. Joshua is the first to see God's handwriting carried by Moses. Scripture does not say how close Joshua comes to God's cloud of glory during the forty days it surrounds Moses on top of the mountain, but he never forgets that incredible experience. Now, God is calling Joseph to step from practice into reality. Joshua has seen and observed; now it is time to lead and conquer in the strength of the Lord's might.

Another parallel between Moses and Joshua is that they both began their leadership at about eighty years old. By the grace of God, both men could recall the faith-strengthening decades of experience seeing God lead His people.

Forging through the hard knocks of life knowing that God leads the charge strengthens our faith.

**How have you seen that truth in your life?**

Knowing God through His Word is key. God specifically reminds Joshua to meditate on His Word day and night. In a literal sense, meditating looks like mulling it over. It looks like chewing it over and over like a cow chewing cud. Just think of how many times a day God brings His Word to your mind and you mull it over to yourself.

What do these passages say about meditating on God's Word?

**Psalm 1:2**

**Psalm 119:15**

**Psalm 119:148**

Knowing God's Word is only half of the equation. Being careful to do what it commands is the other half—and is, perhaps, more difficult. Jesus says to forgive as He forgives, to love your enemies, and to turn the other cheek. None of that is easy, but all of it is commanded. By the grace of God through faith, He gives us the strength to follow Him and His commands. Just as He does with Joshua.

Commissioned by God and blessed by His promises, Joshua now stands ready to step into his leadership role for God's people.

## GO QUIET, GO DEEP

Quiet your mind from distractions and pull your Bible close. Bow your head and ask Jesus to make His Word and today's text personal for you.

Take your time writing out Psalm 91:9–10.

What does it mean to you to make the Lord your dwelling place?

I pray that God's Spirit that is in you continues to strengthen and grow your faith as you rest in His unchanging grace.

Day 4

# JOSHUA ASSUMES COMMAND

*(Joshua 1:10–18)*

When I accepted early retirement in 2021 from the law firm where I had worked for many years, I had a choice. I could find another job or launch into full time as a writer and teacher. I was more than a decade shy of the official retirement age. There would be no steady income from a retirement fund or Social Security when the firm's six-month early retirement package ran out. It was a big decision.

After much time in prayer and pouring through God's Word, I knew it was time to transition into full-time ministry to the church. It was one of the biggest leaps of faith of my entire life. And it has been one of the greatest joys God has ever given to me. One of the requirements to form a 501(c)(3) nonprofit organization is forming a board of directors to govern it. Discerning the godly men and women to walk alongside me to lead this work took much time and prayer. God continues to bless this service a hundredfold because of their godly discernment.

Choosing a leadership team is no small matter. Joshua, though, stepped into a team that was already in place. That scenario presents unique blessings and challenges.

### Joshua's Leadership Team

**Read Joshua 1:10–11. What stands out to you in those verses?**

God does not command Joshua to enter the Promised Land without a leadership team. Joshua inherits from his predecessor a group called "the officers of the people." They first appear in Numbers 11:16–17 when elders were appointed to aid Moses. The appointed leaders appear again in Deuteronomy 1:9–18.

Godly leadership is a unifying thread in Scripture:

> The theme of leadership for God's people, begun in the Pentateuch, continues through Joshua. It will culminate in the ministry of Jesus Christ and will continue in the ministries of the apostles, pastors, and other servants of the Word in the church until Christ comes again.[1]

Joshua faced a challenge that is common to any new company or ministry leader: working with existing staff to forge a good working relationship and keep tasks moving forward.

**If you have stepped into any leadership role with an existing team, what did you find most challenging? What was the biggest blessing?**

Although we do not know how long each member of Moses' team had been serving, chances are some were long-tenured. Perhaps some of them liked the old way of doing things. In a bid to stay relevant in their respective leadership roles, they may have pointed out difficulties with Joshua's new way of doing things. Joshua could easily interpret such suggestions as resistance to God's vision for the future.

Joshua faces another challenge: keeping the balance between their task of conquering cities and the greater task of maintaining their devotion to the Lord. Each of us today faces the same challenge as we serve the Lord in our called vocation—whether in the church or in the world.

As any leader knows, new leadership can be like walking a tightrope. Joshua needs both God's supernatural power and the leaders' support in order to conquer the Promised Land. He has proven to be capable and faithful, but Moses is certainly a tough act to follow.

The leadership transition from Elijah to Elisha comes to mind. Elijah was a prophetic icon, but God did not ask Elisha to be just like him. Each was unique and different even though they shared striking similarities in ministry and mannerisms. Elijah's miracles were grand in scope and spectacle, whereas Elisha's miracles were more low key, using everyday items like water and axe heads. Elijah thrived alone in the wilds, whereas Elisha enjoyed the company of students and prophets.

Such contrast between Elijah and Elisha and between Moses and Joshua teaches an important lesson. In leadership succession, we may be tempted to measure our success or failure against our predecessor's record.

**Have you been tempted to do that? If so, what happened?**

God gives each of us unique gifts and callings. He never asks us to be like anyone other than Christ. God has prepared you and me for this time and place. The last thing we want to do is limit God's work through us by copying the ministry of our predecessors. A godly, bold leader constantly strives to discover new ways to share the Gospel message with a changing world while staying faithful to God's Word.

If God had wanted Joshua to be like Moses, God would have kept Moses in his leadership role. But in Joshua, God brings new blood, vigor, and military gifts to the table. And God would leverage them accordingly.

**What God-given gifts do you bring to the table to share God's Word with others?**

I have a God-given passion for studying Scripture. I have been told that holy passion is evident every time God opens doors for me to teach His Word. Since I did not know Jesus until I was in my twenties, I remember how dark and desperate my life was without Him. I am passionate about others coming to know Jesus through His Word. But the key is knowing God's Word.

God reminds Joshua to meditate on the Book of the Law day and night so he can carefully walk in it. The only way that believers can walk obediently in God's perfect plan is to study God's Word, know it intimately, and live our lives in obedience to it. That's how God prepares Joshua (and us) for success.

**In this season of life, when do you find time to spend in God's Word?**

Whether five minutes or five hours, no amount of time you spend in God's Word is ever wasted. The more time you spend studying, the better you know just how much the Lord loves and cares for you.

**In Joshua 1:11, what does Joshua instruct the leaders to tell the people?**

Joshua wants the people to be ready with provisions such as food and necessary supplies to cross the Jordan successfully and conquer the Promised Land. Readiness is crucial when following God.

**What does Jesus instruct in Luke 12:35–36?**

Like God's people in Joshua's day, we are to be ready as God's people today. The most important provision is the faith given to us by the Holy Spirit to trust God every step of the journey.

## Rest

**Read Joshua 1:12–13.**

There is an important word that we may skip right over as we follow the exciting ramp-up of the storyline. Let's pause here to fill in that particular word from Joshua 1:13:

**"The Lord your God is providing you a place of ________________ and will give you this land."**

God pairs possession of the land with rest. Many battles await God's people as they cross over, so God reminds them to rest. Rest is part of the inheritance God promised from the beginning. Take a moment to write out these verses:

**Deuteronomy 12:10**

**Deuteronomy 25:19**

As New Testament believers, we are invited to rest in Christ. Those are welcome words for a weary soul—especially in this day and age. One of the most important things God teaches His people when He liberates them from Egyptian slavery is to set aside a day of rest. They had become accustomed to seven-day work weeks and their worth amounting to how many bricks they produced.

Read and write out these soul-soothing verses:

**Matthew 11:28–30**

**Hebrews 4:9–11**

**When it comes to resting in the Lord, how are you doing?**

Our rest in Christ is not only a physical rest but a spiritual refueling. It is vital to take a day to step off the hamster wheel to breathe. To worship God.

To receive the Lord's Supper and refuel your soul. To do something you love. To simply be with Him in His Word. If you work weekends, it does not matter which day of the week you rest. Just be sure to set one aside. The blessings are indescribable.

### Issuing Instructions

**Read Joshua 1:14–18.**

We do not know if Joshua is uncomfortable issuing commands without Moses shouldering the repercussions. But God strengthens Joshua to trust in Him completely and rely on Him for everything the people need. As Joshua issues instructions, he issues a special command.

**Look back at Joshua 1:12. Who is Joshua addressing?**

**In Joshua 1:14, what does he command them?**

It may come as a surprise that not all the Israelites will choose to live in Canaan. The Reubenites, Gadites, and the half-tribe of Manasseh had asked Moses to remain on the east side of the Jordan instead of crossing over. With ample grazing and pastureland, these shepherding tribes thought it was ideally suited. The Lord granted their request.

Consequently, after forty years of wandering in the desert, those two and one-half tribes are already enjoying their God-given rest. Even though the tribes of Reuben, Gad, and the half-tribe of Manasseh had made their regrettable choice to not enter the Promised Land, it would not change God's command through Moses to help their brethren. Joshua reminds them of their promise to Moses.

After forty years, the children of those who grumbled at Moses in the desert are now stepping up to make better choices. The Lord raised up a new generation and the change is noticeable. They learned valuable lessons from their parents' mistakes and are inspired to be faithful to God and His plan.

May the same be said of us.

## GO QUIET, GO DEEP

Quiet your mind from distractions and pull your Bible close. Bow your head and ask Jesus to make His Word and today's text personal for you.

Take your time writing out Mark 6:31.

What does it look like to you to get away for rest and quiet time with the Lord?

I pray that you serve the Lord with every ounce of the strength He gives you, then take time to rest one day each week so that He can refuel you for the next stage in your faith journey.

## DAY 5

# RAHAB HIDES THE SPIES

*(Joshua 2)*

Joshua faces many tasks as he prepares to lead the people across the Jordan into the Promised Land.

In a short time span, we have seen three significant events happen. First, God officially commissioned Joshua. Second, the Israelites pledged their unwavering support of Joshua. And third, Joshua reminded the two and one-half tribes that settled east of the Jordan to keep their promise and help their brethren conquer western Canaan. Now, it is time for some reconnaissance work.

**Read Joshua 2:1.**

Jericho is the nearest large fortified city that they would encounter across the Jordan. As a veteran warrior, Joshua needs to know exactly what awaits them, so he secretly sends two spies.

**Why do you believe Joshua sent them secretly?**

Moses sent Joshua, Caleb, and ten other spies during the years they wandered in the desert to the Promised Land (Numbers 13). On their return, they reported to Moses, Aaron, and all the people what they had seen. Mass hysteria and fear overruled their faith in God's direction, and Moses failed to lead God's people into the land God had promised to them.

**In Numbers 14:6–9, what did Joshua and Caleb report to Moses?**

Joshua does not make the same mistake as Moses did. He keeps the mission secret, limits the number of spies to two, and orders that the report be given directly him and not to the whole assembly. Joshua's fearless faith stands in stark contrast to Moses' indecisive, weak mission decades earlier. Sometimes the greatest lesson we can learn from prior leaders is what not to do.

**Read Joshua 2:2–7.**

Joshua's two spies are the first of God's great caravan to cross the Jordan into enemy territory. They are the first to scale Jericho's mighty walls. There is one big difference between these two spies and the spies Moses sent into Canaan decades before. Joshua's spies are not on a fact-finding mission. Instead, they are previewing the victory God has already prepared for His people.

The spies go straight into the house of a prostitute. Wait, what? It was easy to spot prostitutes in those days because they did not wear a veil to cover their hair or faces so that potential customers could appraise their beauty from the street with a glance.

**Why do you believe that the spies choose Rahab's house?**

The spies are unknown visitors, so entering such an establishment would arouse little suspicion from the locals. Such behavior is similar to the agenda of passing sailors and pirates of old who docked in port towns for a night of revelry before their next long stint at sea. However, the king of Jericho also has spies. They alert him about the presence and mission of the two strangers.

**In Joshua 2:4–6, what does Rahab do?**

We might leap to the conclusion that a lie negates a blessing. However, even though Rahab lies to protect them, we cannot forget how the Hebrew wives in Egypt lied to Pharaoh to preserve Moses' life as an infant (Exodus 1:16–21). God uses courageous faith to battle corrupt systems, even today. And Rahab has faith.

But there is spiritual insight that we cannot miss. Rahab hides the two spies "with the stalks of flax that she had laid up in order on the roof" (Joshua 2:6). In biblical times, linen was made from the long flexible fibers of flax. Linen was used in the priestly garments (Leviticus 16:4) and represented purity. After the crucifixion, Jesus is wrapped in linen cloth before being laid in the tomb. Flax was routinely spun and braided to forge strong ropes as well. Since Rahab is drying flax in the sun on her rooftop, the rope she uses to lower the spies to safety (Joshua 2:15) is likely made from flax. The scarlet cord she places in the window to identify her home when the spies return (Joshua 2:21) is also likely made from flax.

Although we cannot take this analogy too far, the fact that Rahab hides the spies sent by Joshua under stalks of flax provides a beautiful picture of God's protection on a whole different level. Rahab works by faith understanding that her hope rests in God alone.

**Read Joshua 2:8–14. Why do you believe Rahab risks her life for complete strangers?**

Long before Joshua's spies show up inside Jericho's fortified walls, the Spirit of the living God had already been there. God had moved in the heart and mind of this woman. Today, Christians and missionaries might believe God's Spirit and His Word show up only when they do. But to believe that is to limit God through a lack of understanding of who He is and His mission.

**Have you ever believed that God showed up only in certain situations when you did? If so, what happened?**

God uses the faith of a prostitute to protect Joshua's spies in Jericho. Rahab appears on the pages of Scripture for the first time here in Joshua 2. Notably, she is mentioned more often in the New Testament than in Joshua. In fact, the "Hall of Faith" in Hebrews memorializes Rahab's great faith, yet Joshua is conspicuously absent.

**Write out Hebrews 11:31.**

The truth that we are saved by faith and not by works is abundantly evident in Rahab's situation. Rahab was clearly saved by grace and faith, not by her profession or pedigree.

**What does James 2:25–26 tell us?**

We are saved by faith, but that does not excuse us from the work of God. Receiving God's incredible gift of faith does not grant us a license to coast through life pursuing the things of this world. That gift comes with great responsibility.

Rahab was saved by faith and works to save her family from destruction. She is one of five women mentioned in Matthew's genealogy of Christ (Matthew 1:5). From her lineage came King David and Jesus Christ. God had plans for Rahab before time began, just like He has plans for you and me. We have much to learn from Rahab's faith, despite her profession.

**Have you ever had to take a significant risk to save your family from harm? If so, what happened?**

Rahab's sense of urgency reveals that perhaps she knows God's destruction of Jericho is imminent. She had heard the stories of what God had done for His people, and she believes them. We know this because she recites a few of the stories to Joshua's two spies.

Now, with God's people gathered just across the Jordan preparing to cross over, Rahab leaps into action and puts her life at risk to save herself and her family.

**Read Joshua 2:15–21.**

Not only does Rahab hide Joshua's spies and mislead their pursuers, but she also possesses street smarts. She knows the lay of the land. She knows precisely which hills the spies need to hide in and for how long.

**In Joshua 2:18, what do the spies promise Rahab?**

The Israelite spies ease Rahab's mind by telling her precisely how they will help rescue her and her family from destruction. Since Joshua and the spies would have been able to see the scarlet cord hanging from her window as they entered the land, this tells us that Rahab likely lives within a chamber of Jericho's wall itself. Old Testament city defensive walls were often several feet thick, so this occurrence was not uncommon. Consequently, from her outer window, one scarlet cord would signal the rescue location.

> The fact that Rahab's family is kept safe in the house marked by the scarlet cord may also remind us of the first Passover, forty years earlier in Egypt, when the blood of a lamb on the doorposts and lintel marked and saved the families of Israel from the death of the firstborn. It may also remind us of our eternal safety in the church, the household of God, through the blood of Jesus Christ.[2]

Christ alone is our source of eternal rescue. He lived the perfect life that we could not, died to forgive our sins for all time, and rose victoriously to prepare a place for us in heaven. The scarlet thread of His love woven through our lives makes an eternal difference.

**Read Joshua 2:22–24.**

With Rahab's help, the mission of the spies is successful. They return to Joshua to report all they had seen and experienced.

**In Joshua 2:24, what do the spies tell Joshua?**

Their faith in God and exuberance to do all the Lord had commanded them is reminiscent of Joshua and Caleb's report to Moses decades earlier. Specifically, they tell Joshua that "all the inhabitants of the land melt away because of us." The enemies of Israel across the river are melting in fear of the Lord.

**When was the last time you were truly excited about stepping into a plan that God laid out before you? What happened?**

God gives us the faith to trust Him even in the hardest circumstances. Like He did for the spies and Rahab, He provides the assurance we need to do His will with wholehearted trust that He walks with us every step of the journey.

## GO QUIET, GO DEEP

Quiet your mind from distractions and pull your Bible close. Bow your head and ask Jesus to make His Word and today's text personal for you.

Take your time writing out 2 Timothy 1:7.

What does it mean to you to operate in God's strength and power since we have not been given a spirit of fear?

I pray that God inspires you to risk all He has given you (like Rahab) to share His message of salvation to the ends of the earth.

LESSON 2

# God Will Make a Way

*Joshua 3:1–5:12*

As Joshua leads the Israelites into the Promised Land, God instructs the Levitical priests to carry the ark of the covenant at the vanguard of their march across the Jordan. God's presence faithfully goes before His people to ensure that they cross the Jordan on dry ground.

Just as they entered the Promised Land at long last, God reinstitutes the rite of circumcision and the Israelites observe the Passover. Neither had been kept up while they wandered through the desert under Moses' leadership. God's presence among His people is the integral, vital key to safely arriving in the Promised Land.

Today, Jesus is the only way you and I will arrive safely past enemy lines into the promised land of eternity to reign with Him.

DAY 1: Joshua Prepares God's People to Cross the Jordan (Joshua 3:1–6)

DAY 2: God's Promises to Joshua (Joshua 3:7–8)

DAY 3: Joshua Imparts God's Word to the People (Joshua 3:9–17)

DAY 4: Twelve Memorial Stones (Joshua 4)

DAY 5: Circumcision and Passover (Joshua 5:1–12)

**Key Questions:**

- What is the biggest leap of faith that the Lord has put before you?
- When God gives you significant victories over life's struggles, how do you honor Him for His faithfulness?

- What spiritual practices do you observe to keep God at the center of your life?

## Day 1

# JOSHUA PREPARES GOD'S PEOPLE TO CROSS THE JORDAN

*(Joshua 3:1–6)*

The day has finally arrived for God's people to enter the Promised Land. What an extraordinary day! They prepare to move their possessions, carrying the promises of God in their hearts to see the land just across the Jordan with their own eyes.

**Read Joshua 3:1.**

Joshua sets a wonderful example of rising early to give God the best energy of his day. If you are an early riser, you understand that fresh, sunrise-fueled energy. On the days I wake up early, I accomplish more before lunchtime than I accomplish all day when I sleep later.

The Israelites are camped at a place called Shittim in the plains of Moab on the east side of the Jordan. It is an area near the Jordan River that some historians believe contained many palm trees and acacia trees. It is a beautiful place of refreshment and a picture of God's provision! The location holds a unique significance for the Israelites. We learned in Joshua 2 that Joshua sent the two spies to survey Jericho from Shittim. However, there is another connection between Shittim and God's people.

**Read Numbers 25:1–5. What did the Israelites do at Shittim?**

When Moses was leading the Israelites through the desert, they committed terrible sin at Shittim and paid for it dearly. Yet now, God brings the Israelites back to the place where they failed terribly to provide rest before leading them into their promised inheritance. What a beautiful display of God's redeeming grace!

What do the following verses say about redemption?

**Ephesians 1:7**

**Psalm 130:7**

**1 Peter 1:18–19**

God alone is our redeemer. He alone will redeem His people to inherit the land He promised to them through Abraham.

Other than Joshua and Caleb, no Israelite who enters the Promised Land is over forty years old. Because of Israel's sin in the desert, God decreed that generation would not enter the Promised Land.

**What does Numbers 14:30–31 tell us?**

Consequently, it is the children of the wanderers who would inherit God's promise. It is a young Israel—who only knew the discipline of the wilderness—that is about to witness God's covenant promise become reality.

They carry no baggage from the "comforts" of slavery. None of them (other than Joshua and Caleb) had lived long in Egypt under Pharaoh. The youth, hope, and enthusiasm that enters the Promised Land are necessary to vigorously conquer and settle it. That generation probably understands better than any other that they literally would not survive without God.

**Read Joshua 3:2–4. Why do you believe it is significant for them to follow the ark of the covenant?**

The ark of the covenant was constructed by the Israelites during their wanderings in the desert (Exodus 25).

> The ark of the covenant, a chest about 3 ¾ feet long and 2 ¼ feet wide. It was made of acacia wood and lined and covered with gold. The solid gold lid of this chest was called the mercy seat. . . . The ark went before Israel in its wilderness journeys "to seek out a resting place for them" ([Numbers] 10:33). Priests carried it into the Jordan River, where it halted the waters so that the people could cross over on dry land into Palestine ([Joshua] 3:11–17).[3]

The ark of the covenant holds great spiritual significance as the manifestation of God's physical presence on earth. The ark is the place where God meets with His people. The cloud of God would rest on the mercy seat of the ark to instruct Moses (Leviticus 16:2; Numbers 7:89).

According to Hebrews 9:4, the ark contains only three items. First, it holds the sacred stone tablets of the Ten Commandments carved by the finger of God that Moses brought down from Mount Sinai (Exodus 31:18). Second, it holds Aaron's rod that budded (Numbers 17). Finally, it holds a bowl of manna which had been Israel's source of food for decades in the desert (Exodus 16:33–34).

Bear in mind that the ark is usually hidden from view. It is kept in the Holy of Holies within the tabernacle. Each time the Israelites move camp, the Levites (the God-appointed priestly caretakers of the ark) are the ones who carefully transport it. Because of the number of people, it is not a stretch to believe that some Israelites may have never actually seen the ark. But now it would be lifted high in full, glorious view as a beacon of hope.

By following the ark across the Jordan, the Israelites are following God. It is important to note that crossing the Jordan River at that point in the exodus is not the most direct route from Egypt into Canaan. But when

Moses and the Israelites did not enter the land after Joshua, Caleb, and the spies gave their report, the people forfeited their right to direct access. In fact, Deuteronomy 1:2 reveals that their original journey from Egypt to the Promised Land should have taken only eleven days.

**Have you ever listened to someone's opinion or story and followed their advice only to discover they were wrong? If so, what happened?**

**How did God work in your situation?**

**How did it impact your spiritual journey?**

While the ark will go before the Israelites, orders are specifically given to keep their distance from it. God cannot coexist in the presence of sin, which is mankind's very nature. However, God is not like a spotless white couch where no one can sit to avoid soiling it. Rather, sin cannot exist in God's presence because the consuming fire of His love and holiness cleanses all sin. God cannot be tainted by our sin any more than the ocean could turn red from one drop of red dye. Sin enslaves and destroys humanity, which is why God took our whole weight of sin upon Himself in Jesus on the cross. By the grace of God, sin vanishes at the slightest touch of God's blazing holiness.

Since no one can look on the presence of God and live (Exodus 33:20), the ark is kept at a safe distance from the Israelites with strict warnings for the distance to be honored. They are to follow it, not touch it.

**Write out the last sentence of Joshua 3:4.**

With each instruction, God affirms that He is leading His people into a place they have never been. What a glorious truth! God does not tell the Israelites or us to go into places He has not prepared. We can certainly choose to go to places outside His will, but He will never send us to places He has not already been. We saw that truth in Rahab's story where God's Spirit had already prepared Rahab's heart to turn to the Lord.

Our lives do not comprise random wanderings. God prepares our way and goes before us in every area of our lives. The job we work, the community in which we live, and the family in which we grew up are not random.

**How have you seen this truth in your life?**

**Does the fact that God goes before you offer comfort or anxiety? Why?**

God has given you the precise life experiences and set your feet today exactly where He has prepared you to be for His glory—both in blessings and challenges.

**Read Joshua 3:5–6. What stands out to you in these verses?**

Even though Israel has yet to take the land, God has effectively handed them the legal title. The Israelites simply wait for God's perfect timing to live in it. The area of land God is giving Israel is vast, diverse, and contains all that His people would need to survive and thrive.

Now it is time to receive the inheritance that God had promised. But first, the people are instructed to consecrate themselves.

**What do you believe it means to consecrate yourself to the Lord?**

The Hebrew word used here for consecrate (*qādaš*) refers to dedicating, preparing, and sanctifying. It means being set apart for God's purposes to live a holy life that honors and brings glory to Him. For the Israelites, consecration would look like separating themselves from anything unclean, fasting, and spending time in worship and prayer.

Once again demonstrating a parallel between Joshua and Moses, this was not the first time the people were instructed to consecrate themselves to the Lord. In Exodus 19:10–11, God instructed Moses on Mount Sinai to tell the people to consecrate themselves to the Lord before God revealed Himself to them. God called the first generation of Israelites to consecrate themselves at Mount Sinai because He was about to visit them. And God calls the second generation to consecrate themselves at the Jordan River because He is about to lead the way—literally—into the Promised Land.

There is an important principle for us here. When we live consecrated to the Lord, we can expect to see Him working and experience His leading in our lives. By the grace of God, all Christians are consecrated and set aside for God.

How do you see that truth in the following verses?

**1 Peter 2:9–10**

**2 Corinthians 6:14–17**

Just as God has set His people apart today, He set them apart in Joshua's day too. Part of being set apart and prepared to serve the Lord is prompt and wholehearted cooperation with His commands.

God can bring about anything in any generation if we keep our eyes on Him and follow Him through the wilderness into His promises.

## GO QUIET, GO DEEP

Quiet your mind from distractions and pull your Bible close. Bow your head and ask Jesus to make His Word and today's text personal for you.

Take your time writing out Isaiah 44:22.

What does it mean to you that you have been fully redeemed by God?

I pray that you never take for granted what the Lord has redeemed you from and redeemed you for.

## Day 2

# GOD'S PROMISES TO JOSHUA

*(Joshua 3:7–8)*

During my five-plus decades of life, I have moved several times. Whether it was moving during childhood when dad's job changed, moving into my first apartment in Houston, or moving into a newlywed condo with my husband, each move has held blessings and challenges. But one particular move stands head and shoulders above all the rest.

In 2018, I bought my first home. I had been divorced eight years by then and still lived in a house in the Houston suburbs that was far too large for just me and my two cats. I searched diligently for months because this next home needed to be just right. The suburban house sold faster than I expected, so rather than make a hasty decision on which home to buy, I moved into an apartment to give myself ample time to keep searching.

Six months later, God provided the perfect home. It checked off all the boxes, including being near my mom and sisters. Plus, its Texas cottage cuteness factor was simply off the charts. Surrounded by more trees than people, the land provided an ample backyard for flower and vegetable gardens and the house was just the right size. Not too big. Not too small. One story with two bedrooms, the larger of which would be my study and writing cave.

When moving day arrived, my excitement was absolutely through the roof! Family and friends showed up to make short work of moving my things and getting everything settled. In the years since then, my little cottage has become an oasis of peace, love, spiritual growth, contentment, and creativity. There is much to be said for simplicity and the simple pleasures in life amid the chaotic confusion of our modern days.

**What has been the most significant move in your life? How has God blessed you through it?**

In today's text, Joshua and the Israelites are poised and ready to cross the Jordan River into the Promised Land. Moving day has finally arrived.

**Read Joshua 3:7–8. What stands out to you in those verses?**

For the second time in the book of Joshua, the Lord directly addresses Joshua. The first time was in Joshua 1, where God encouraged Joshua with a particular phrase repeated three times: "Be strong and courageous."

This time, the Lord has a two-part message for Joshua. The first part is for Joshua; the second part contains instructions for the Israelites. Let's take a closer look at each part.

**Write out Joshua 3:7.**

Before God instructs Joshua regarding what to tell His people corporately, He takes the opportunity to encourage Joshua personally.

**What stands out to you in that verse?**

God's first order of business is to show Joshua (and later His people) that He is faithful. As He was with Moses, so He will be with Joshua. God makes that same promise to be with us today as well. Read and write out the following verses, which confirm that beautiful truth:

**Matthew 1:23**

**John 14:16–17**

**Psalm 145:18**

**As you navigate this season of your life, what comfort does the truth that God is with you bring?**

As Joshua stands at the Jordan River ready to behold yet another great miracle of God, we can only imagine the holy comfort that floods Joshua's soul at the Lord's words. He is not leading in his own strength. He knows beyond a shadow of a doubt that the Lord went before them.

There is one small but vital word in Joshua 3:7 that bears further scrutiny: *begin*. To label something as a beginning means that the rest of the story will follow. It implies that God's promise to exalt Joshua will extend beyond that day's miracle. By the time we reach the end of this study, we will know the series of events that God works to honor Joshua as a leader after His own heart. That day is only the beginning.

It is important to note that God does not say He would exalt Joshua for Joshua's glory. God exalts Joshua so that the people would trust and follow Joshua and then together give God the glory for His faithfulness.

**Write out Joshua 3:8.**

This second part of the Lord's instructions to Joshua addresses the priests' role in God's second great water-crossing miracle.

As the God-appointed caretakers of the ark, the priests would take the ark and stand still in the Jordan. Did you catch that? The priests would not be crossing over into Canaan to wait for the multitude to join them. The priests would be standing IN the Jordan as the people crossed. We will revisit that detail later during the Israelites' actual river crossing.

**Has God ever urged you to stand (or take a stand) for His glory somewhere unusual or uncomfortable? If so, on what occasion? What happened?**

Sometimes, the most uncomfortable place that God asks a believer to stand is to stand up for the truth of the Gospel and share the love of Jesus with those who may be hostile to His message. Perhaps He has nudged you to stand up for truth when those around you urge you to be deceptive. Maybe the Lord has urged you to stand firm on the promises of God when the enemy whispers doubts.

Following God is crucial because He takes us to places we have never been—much like the Israelites. The first command for God's people in Joshua 3:3 is extraordinarily simple: Keep your eyes on the ark. The command for us today is extraordinarily simple: Keep our eyes fixed on Jesus, the author and perfecter of our faith (Hebrews 12:2). Even though the command is simple, faithfully following it can become extraordinarily hard when we start getting ahead of God and His plans for us.

Joshua now stands ready to lead God's people into the Promised Land with the Lord's instructions ringing fresh in his heart and mind.

The ark would move, so God's people would move with it. The ark would be lifted high as a faith-strengthening, visible reminder of God's covenant promises. And He who promised them would be faithful.

## GO QUIET, GO DEEP

Quiet your mind from distractions and pull your Bible close. Bow your head and ask Jesus to make His Word and today's text personal for you.

Take your time writing out Ephesians 6:13.

What does it mean to you to "stand firm" wherever the Lord places you today?

I pray that through the faith given to you by God and the strength of His Holy Spirit inside of you, that you never shrink from standing firm in the Lord.

## DAY 3

# JOSHUA IMPARTS GOD'S WORD TO THE PEOPLE

*(Joshua 3:9–17)*

History has shown that Winston Churchill was one of the greatest leaders of the twentieth century. Leading up to World War II, Churchill remained vigilant about Hitler's movements and paid close attention to intercepted messages that revealed Hitler's intentions to occupy all of Europe.

As prime minister of the United Kingdom during the war, Churchill delivered several legendary wartime speeches. He was a gifted orator and used words to inspire and lead with excellence. On June 4, 1940, during one of his most famous addresses to the House of Commons, Churchill said, "We shall fight on the beaches, we shall fight on the landing grounds, we shall fight in the fields and in the streets, we shall fight in the hills; we shall never surrender."[4]

People trusted Churchill's wisdom because he possessed accurate information, appropriate strategies, and sufficient manpower to prevent Hitler from conquering England.

A strong leader who wholeheartedly strives toward a common goal without flinching is inspiring and necessary. God made Joshua such a leader.

**Read Joshua 3:9. What stands out to you in that verse?**

Joshua wants to ensure that he has the people's undivided attention before communicating the Lord's command to Israel. Picture an elementary school teacher who holds up one hand to get the students' attention while putting the other hand over his or her mouth to signal the students to be quiet.

Notably, this is the first time in the book of Joshua where Joshua tells the people that the instructions they are about to receive are "the words of the LORD."

**Why is that significant?**

By communicating "the words of the LORD" to the Israelites, Joshua functions as a prophet. Even though Scripture never labels Joshua as such, his role to be God's spokesperson to the Israelites defines the role of a prophet.

Again, there is one significant phrase we cannot miss in Joshua 3:9: "the LORD your God." Joshua reminds them that He is their God. The One who established a covenant relationship with them. The One who has sustained them all the way to the Jordan River.

God is our God as well. He is my God. He is *your* God, so draw near because you do not want to miss a word He has said.

**Take a moment to read Psalm 139:1–18. From these verses, write out every way you see that God knows you.**

The God of the universe and Creator of all things knows you personally and loves you immeasurably. Not one struggle you face or joy you experience escapes His mighty gaze. And because of Jesus' voluntary sacrifice on the cross and glorious resurrection, one day you will see Him face to face to behold those truths in person.

**Read Joshua 3:10–13.**

Now that Joshua has their full attention, he tells the Israelites the Lord's instructions. Historians estimate that at this point at the end of their exodus, the Israelites numbered more than two million people. That's hard for our minds to grasp. Imagine that a standard National Football League stadium seats around 75,000. Now multiply that to about thirty stadiums side-by-side and the picture becomes clearer.

Joshua specifically mentions the seven people groups that the Israelites would face in the Promised Land.

**Who are those seven nations listed in Joshua 3:10?**

Although seven nations are listed, that number is merely a representation that encompasses all of Israel's enemies upon whom God has pronounced judgment. The number *seven* throughout Scripture often refers to the number of divine completion. In fact, the apostle Paul notes in his sermon at Antioch in Pisidia (Acts 13:19) the "seven nations in the land of Canaan" mentioned here (and in Deuteronomy 7:1) that God overthrew. Bible scholars draw a parallel between their destruction in history and the destruction of Judgment Day:

> This destruction was a sign of God's eschatological wrath against sin, which will be fully displayed after the return of Jesus Christ and the end of this present world. Thus the destruction of these seven peoples may be compared to the destruction and judgment of Babylon . . . and the eternal damnation of all unbelievers on Judgment Day (Revelation 20).[5]

The Canaanites, Hittites, Hivites, Girgashites, Jebusites, and Amorites descended from Noah's grandson Canaan, the son of Ham (Genesis 10:15–17). They are wicked and idolatrous people far from God. Not much is known about the Perizzites apart from the fact that they live in forestland (Joshua 17:15). The Jebusites inhabit mountainous regions, but Jerusalem is their city (Joshua 15:63). They are warriors who maintain control of Jerusalem until the era of King David.

**In Joshua 3:11, what specific assurance does Joshua provide to show the Israelites that the living God is among them as they go into the Promised Land?**

The people know that the Lord's presence rests on the mercy seat of the ark of the covenant. Where the ark went, God's presence surely is there. God has faithfully led them for forty years through the desert; He would not abandon them now that their inheritance is in sight.

One of the things I struggled with the most when I became a Christian was that I could not physically see God. That was especially true when it came to prayer. It felt like I was praying to thin air. How reassuring it must have been for the Israelites to have the ark as a visible spectacle of the living God on display right before their eyes!

**Why do you believe that it is important for the Israelites to know that God is a "living" God?**

The land they enter is full of idol-worshiping Canaanites who carve their gods from wood and stone. Lifeless, empty, and worthless. The living God wants His people to see Him as an active agent in their salvation: living, active, and guiding them with His great love.

**In Joshua 3:13, where are the priests instructed to stand?**

We touched on this briefly in our last session. For God to hold back the Jordan River, the priests first have to step into the water as they carry the ark.

**Why is that an important detail?**

Throughout Scripture, God reminds us that we are to walk by faith. God has given us the faith to believe, but it is up to us to actively walk in it.

**How do you see that truth in the following verses?**

**2 Corinthians 5:7**

**Galatians 2:20**

Jesus knocks at the door. He does not break it down and force us to live by faith. His Spirit gives us the strength and courage to follow Him faithfully.

**How are you putting your feet in the raging waters of our modern turbulent times to walk by faith?**

Read Joshua 3:14–17.

According to biblical maps, the Jordan River began just below Mount Hermon and flowed south into the Sea of Galilee and then the Dead Sea. Joshua and the Israelites are located just north of the Dead Sea and east of Jericho.

I have been blessed to stand in the Jordan River on several occasions during my teaching tours to the Holy Land. For the majority of the year, the Jordan is a calm three feet deep and forty feet wide at its smallest point, and ten feet deep and one hundred feet wide at its largest. It is certainly a pleasant, cool place to stand on a hot desert day. On this day though, as the Israelites are preparing to cross, the Jordan is at flood stage during harvest season. The raging water is thundering over its banks and roaring rapidly. Definitely not a pleasant place to stand. Only the mighty hand of God could part it in such a way to make it safe for His people to traverse. Holding back the Jordan River is a stunning display of God's mighty power.

This brings to mind an interesting nuance. No Israelite other than Joshua and Caleb had witnessed God's great miracle of the Red Sea crossing. No one else had seen Moses hold up his staff and the waters of the Red Sea part before them.

Like Moses, Joshua has now come up against an obstacle of water that stands between Israel and the place God instructed them to go. Moses faced the Red Sea. Joshua faces the Jordan River. Neither faces the obstacle without God's miracle-working presence.

God chooses the dangerous flood stage season to command His people to cross the Jordan River. Entering the Promised Land is a huge challenge, yet God adds another layer. He wants their crossing to maximize His glory by demonstrating that they could not have crossed apart from His direct intervention.

Compare this to Lazarus falling sick. Jesus could have healed a sick friend, but God adds another layer. Lazarus dies. God wants the resurrection of Lazarus to maximize Jesus' glory by solidifying that God alone has the power to raise the dead.

But remember that neither Joshua nor Moses face their aqua obstacles alone. God faithfully leads and guides them every step of the way. And not even their sandals get wet.

**Is there an obstacle in your life now that you are weary of trying to overcome by your own strength? If so, how has that worked out?**

We often become weary when we stubbornly choose to fight battles in our own strength that only Christ can conquer in His. For years I fought in my own weakness before knowing Jesus. Even lifelong Christians can struggle to remember to lean on Him. I get it. Taking matters into your own hands is a hard lesson to unlearn. Maybe you have chosen to walk a journey alone that was meant to be walked alongside someone. True rest and ultimate victory can be found only in Christ.

Each of us is born as a slave to sin. Like the Israelites in Egypt, there is no hope for freedom without God's direct intervention. As God led His people out of Egypt into the Promised Land, Jesus leads us today in victory over doubt, sin, and defeat.

God's children could not successfully cross the raging Jordan without God's direct leading and intervention. Yet God places a test of faith in their path. The priests are required to put their feet into the floodwaters of the Jordan before the waters recede.

Such reliance on God before advancing still holds true for Christians today. We cannot enter into what God wants us to possess until we know how to follow His lead. Sensitivity to the presence and movement of God is essential for moving into the plan He has prepared for us. It is the epitome of Psalm 16:8—"I have set the Lord always before me."

Joshua did not direct operations from afar. He was right in the middle of it alongside everyone else. Likewise, Jesus did not direct our salvation operation from afar—He led the charge. Fully God, Jesus knew that the enemy of sin was too big, too strong, and too numerous for mankind to face. Therefore, fully man, Jesus left everything behind to come down from heaven and lead us into battle on earth.

Through the power of the Holy Spirit, He still leads us each and every day. He personally guaranteed our victory through the cross. In Christ, we have a leader who we can follow anywhere and everywhere.

What river rages in your life right now? Do sin, addiction, spiritual failure, and the muddy waters of fear rage around you? Like Joshua, fix your eyes on God! Confess, repent, and follow God by faith across the raging flood.

## GO QUIET, GO DEEP

Quiet your mind from distractions and pull your Bible close. Bow your head and ask Jesus to make His Word and today's text personal for you.

Take your time writing out Psalm 107:29.

What does it mean to you that the Lord will take you safely through the perils of life into His promises?

As the Israelites kept their eyes on the ark of the covenant, I pray that you keep your eyes on the Lord when the waters of life rage around you.

## DAY 4

# TWELVE MEMORIAL STONES

*(Joshua 4)*

My dad served in the U.S. Air Force during the Korean War. My uncle O.J. flew a B-17 Flying Fortress in the Air Force in World War II. And my uncle Johnny served in the Air Force during the Vietnam War. We are very much an Air Force family.

When my dad and two uncles passed, they were buried in veterans' cemeteries in Texas, Arkansas, and Alabama. My dad is laid to rest in Houston National Cemetery, a beautifully manicured location with green rolling hills, ponds, and thousands of military graves.

My relatives' grave markers represent a memorial to their life, faithful military service, and commitment to a cause greater than themselves. There is much to be said for having a physical reminder of faithfulness that can be seen and touched.

Joshua and God's people have successfully crossed over the Jordan River on dry ground. Now the time has come to erect a physical memorial to their faithful God. For the third time in this book, God gives specific instructions to Joshua.

**Read Joshua 4:1–3. What does God command Joshua to do?**

God commands each tribe to carry a stone out of the Jordan (Joshua 4:2) and bring it into the Promised Land as a twelve-stone ebenezer (see 1 Samuel 7:12) reminder of God's faithfulness to the generations to come. Joshua had instructed each tribe to select one man, but the reason was not given. Here, the reason is revealed.

**Where exactly are the twelve stones to be taken from in the Jordan?**

The twelve men are not to simply choose twelve random stones but are specifically to take them "from the very place where the priests' feet stood firmly."

**Why is that detail is important?**

Not only did God want the Israelites to remember that they crossed the Jordan River at flood stage; He wanted them to remember WHO it was that brought their success. The priests held the ark of the covenant as the people crossed over the Jordan on dry ground. Now that the ark is safe across the Jordan, God directs the men to choose stones from exactly where the priests stood as they held the visible reminder of His presence among them.

Notice that Joshua 4:3 says, "Take twelve stones from *here* out of the midst of the Jordan" (emphasis added). The phrasing of the Lord's instruction to Joshua indicates that God is speaking from the ark of the covenant itself in the middle of the Jordan. God's holy presence is still holding back the raging waters to protect the twelve men instructed to gather the stones.

That makes the hair on my arms stand up and my knees buckle! God stands with us in the middle of life's raging floods to hold back danger even when we cannot physically see Him. AMAZING!

For you and me today, Jesus stands faithfully in the middle of our storms to protect us from the ravages of this sinful world.

Write the following verses that affirm this beautiful truth:

**2 Thessalonians 3:3**

**Psalm 46:1**

**Isaiah 41:10**

**Psalm 32:7**

As God calls us to step out in His name into the raging waters of this life, we can be confident that He is there with us and protecting us. Jesus' disciples experience that truth firsthand when Jesus calms the wind and waves in their storm-tossed boat (Mark 4:35–41; Matthew 8:23–27).

**Read Joshua 4:4–8. Why does God specifically instruct them to choose twelve stones?**

God could have used one stone, but He chooses one stone per tribe. God wants the people to remember generations later that He was not only faithful to His people as a whole but to each tribe of the sons of Israel and their descendants. He wants a lasting reminder standing before His people that His love, provision, and mighty movements are equal and personal. Those stones would serve as teachable moments about God's faithfulness.

Erecting stone memorials to commemorate acts of God is not unique to the book of Joshua.

**Read 1 Samuel 7:10–12. What is the stone called that Samuel set up?**

In Hebrew, the word *ebenezer* means "stone of help." Even though the stones erected by Joshua and the Israelites are not referred to as ebenezers, the principle is the same. The raised stones serve as a powerful, visible reminder to the Israelites of what the Lord has done for them.

**Do you have an ebenezer in your life to remind yourself of God's faithfulness?**

I have two special items that serve as ebenezers in my life. When I was baptized at age 23, I was given a candle standing on a wooden base bearing a cross and the baptismal cloth that Pastor Graumann used to wipe my forehead after my Baptism. More than thirty years later, those beautiful ebenezers still sit in a prominent place on a shelf in my study as powerful reminders of God's faithfulness. He gave me the gift of faith, washed my scarlet sins white as snow through Jesus' blood shed on the cross, and snatched me from the jaws of hell to redeem my life for His glory.

Even if that cross and cloth are lost or destroyed someday, what Jesus did for me on the cross stands for all eternity. The stones that Joshua set up at Gilgal are likely buried beneath many centuries of river silt, but it does not change what God does for the Israelites as He leads them into the Promised Land.

**Read Joshua 4:9–14. What stands out to you in this passage?**

Joshua takes the twelve stones gathered by the representatives of the twelve tribes and places them exactly where the feet of the priests stood as they held the ark over the Jordan's dry ground.

The end of verse 10 makes me smile because it says that the people pass over the Jordan "in haste." There is such a human element in those words. Reminiscent of the proverbial Dutch boy with his finger in the dam, did they think that the waters would suddenly be released to drown them before God got them across safely?

Perhaps the people remember a similar water miracle story passed down from their parents. When God parted the Red Sea for Moses, the people passed over on dry ground. However, when they had all crossed, God released the waters as Pharaoh's army pursued after the people. Pharaoh's entire army drowned, including horses and chariots.

More likely, the truth of the situation is that without anything to impede their progress across the Jordan, God's people moved purposefully and diligently into the Promised Land. After all, they had waited a long time for this day.

When the people have all passed through, Joshua finally commands the priests bearing the ark to come out of the Jordan.

**According to Joshua 4:12–13, who passes through the Jordan ahead of the people?**

The fighting men of the two and one-half tribes who had already been settled east of the Jordan for over a year had promised to cross over with the rest of God's people to conquer Canaan.

> While the land of Canaan is a gift freely given by the Lord, he has chosen to employ the army of his covenant nation as his visible agent of victory. The terms "military formations," "armed for battle," and "for the war" (4:12–13) anticipate the coming conquest. . . . Israel has nothing to fear as it acts in the obedience of faith demonstrated here by its eastern tribes.[6]

It is a beautiful picture of one body of believers united under God.

**Read Joshua 4:15–24. What stands out to you in these passages?**

As soon as the priests' feet leave the Jordan's dry ground, the Jordan River rages back to where it was before. What a sight that must have been! Picture the scene in your mind. The 40,000 armed troops have passed over, all of God's people made it through, and the priests have now brought the ark to shore. Imagine the thunderous sound as the river's raging water rushes back where they had just walked!

Our five senses preserve memories that can be triggered later in life by similar events. The Israelites likely never forgot the sight and sound of those waters thundering past them as they finally stood in the land that God had promised to them so long ago.

Then Joshua commands that twelve stones be set up near Gilgal where they camped for the first time in Canaan.

**Summarize in your own words what Joshua tells the people in Joshua 4:23–24.**

God had made Joshua an incredible leader. Without hesitation or debate, he ordered the priests to step into the Jordan's raging currents. Joshua was not focused on the raging flood but on their faithful Redeemer.

And even though God exalted Joshua once again, Joshua does not shout empty bravado or demand self-aggrandizing praise after their crossing. He tells the people to raise twelve ebenezers to the glory of God. Joshua wholly put His faith in God Almighty to provide a path through the impossible. And all worship and praise rightfully belongs solely to the Lord.

What God had done for His people would be passed down from generation to generation. And because of the book of Joshua, we continue to see God's faithfulness to His people today.

By faith, we believe that God brought us to where we stand today. He sustains and preserves us here. And He alone will lead us forward from here past the raging floods we are wading through. To God be the glory!

## GO QUIET, GO DEEP

Quiet your mind from distractions and pull your Bible close. Bow your head and ask Jesus to make His Word and today's text personal for you.

Take your time writing out Romans 8:38–39.

What does it mean to you that the Lord helps you through life's ebbs and flows?

I pray that you take the time to raise an ebenezer to the Lord in a specific place where He has shown Himself faithful to you.

## DAY 5

# CIRCUMCISION AND PASSOVER

*(Joshua 5:1–12)*

Footprints, hoof marks, and imprints of twelve river rocks are quickly covered by the Jordan River's muddy rush as the nation of Israel sets down its feet on the fresh soil of Canaan.

By the grace of God, they had passed from tragedy to triumph, desert to delight. Now, forty years after God liberated them from Egypt, they pitch camp for the first time in the land God had promised to Abraham.

The only thing God wants in return is for His chosen people to worship and serve Him with all their heart, soul, mind, and strength. They are to act as an example of how serving the living God truly means salvation.

As we dive into chapter 5, note that the chapter serves as an important interlude between two distinct sections of the book of Joshua. This chapter highlights the transition from God's people entering the land to their conquest of it.

**Read Joshua 5:1. What is the response of the land's inhabitants to Israel's crossing?**

The miraculous crossing of the Jordan is not only experienced by Israel. Word reaches the pagan Canaanite kings and their people. God desires no ambiguity in identifying the truth about Canaan's new inhabitants: The Israelites are His people, protected by His power. And they are coming.

**According to Joshua 4:24, what is God's purpose for their miraculous crossing?**

As the people set up camp on Canaanite land, notice that it is the *kings* of the Amorites—not the ordinary man—that are now melting like wax. Can you imagine what they must be thinking? *If a raging river cannot stop the Lord, how can we*?

This question brings Jesus' resurrection to mind. The New Testament Pharisees and teachers of the Law must have been just as terrified when they learned that Jesus had risen from the dead. But their terror contains an added twist: They were the ones who demanded Jesus be put to death. Nothing, including death, can stop the power of God Almighty.

The power and working of God in our lives today is not just for us; rather, it is often the way God shows others His glory through our circumstances.

**How has God specifically worked past your circumstances to point others to Him?**

That question is easy for me to answer. Moving from someone who did not even know Jesus to someone who now writes Bible studies and teaches others about who He is and what He has done is solely by the power and grace of God alone. If someone had told me at age 23 what the Lord was equipping me to do today, I would have thought she had lost every single marble in her head.

One of the most intriguing aspects about Israel crossing the Jordan River is that their arrival, successful crossing, and subsequent encampment are never met with opposing military forces. No person, army, or Canaanite king show up to stop the Israelites' crossing. Israel has no chariots or horses. They only have families, livestock, and household goods. The Israelites could easily be slaughtered. But they are not, because the Lord of hosts protects them every step of the way by putting fear in the hearts of their enemies.

**According to Ephesians 6:10–18, what protection has God given to believers today?**

Not only does God's presence live inside every believer through the power of the Holy Spirit, but God has provided us His armor of light for our day-to-day battles in this world.

**Read Joshua 5:2–9. What does God command Joshua to do?**

Before the Israelites look forward, God directs them to look back. God commands Joshua to renew the covenant of circumcision, which had not been observed by Moses during the desert wandering.

Let's take a moment to look at this startling turn of events from a military standpoint. God's people are now camped in enemy territory. One of the most formidable walled cities and its capable soldiers stand not far away. And God's first instruction after crossing over will immediately incapacitate every fighting male among the Israelites.

**Why do you believe God would command circumcision at this point?**

God had settled their physical position in the Promised Land, and now it is time to put their spiritual affairs in order.

**In Genesis 17:1–14, what does God's covenant of circumcision represent?**

God instituted circumcision with Abraham back in Genesis. Circumcision is the physical sign or mark of God's solemn, unbreakable covenant with His people. Circumcision uniquely recognizes a man's pledge as a covenant person under God's divine authority rather than his own free will. It still does today.

Perhaps one of the great disobediences of a rebellious Israel, as they wandered in the desert, is their deliberate refusal to circumcise their male children for forty years. Since they do not view themselves as God's covenant people nor respect Yahweh as their covenant God, they are sentenced to die in the desert.

Consequently, during this interlude between crossing and conquering, while their enemies still tremble in fear, God's people renew their covenant of circumcision. Having already been circumcised forty years before, Joshua understands the enormous risk for Israel to be circumcised. They would be utterly vulnerable to attack, yet Joshua carries out the Lord's command without hesitation.

As God instructs Joshua to prepare flint knives to perform the circumcisions, there is no hint of reproach or reprimand from the Lord. This is simply the next step the Lord put in place for His covenant people to inherit the land He promised to them.

**According to Romans 2:28–29, what does circumcision accomplish for believers today?**

Circumcision is the work of God on a believer's heart, male and female. Through faith, He consecrates us to a spiritual life centered in Him.

**How has God's circumcision of your heart impacted your faith walk?**

**Read Joshua 5:10–12.**

Precisely forty years to the day after Israel celebrated its first Passover in Egypt, they celebrate the Passover together again as God's people. We cannot underestimate the power of that moment. This is the first time in four decades that God's people experience what Moses and their parents experienced in Egypt. I wonder if they share stories passed down from their moms or dads about that night when death passed over every home whose doorpost was marked with lamb's blood. Even today, circumcision and the Passover hold great significance:

> The two great covenants of the Lord with Israel are in view through circumcision and the Passover, the two main ceremonies associated with those covenants. . . . Circumcision was a sign of God's covenant with Abraham, and the Passover celebrated the exodus and Mosaic covenant. The covenant nation had lived in a state of suspension during the thirty-eight years of wandering in the wilderness. They did not circumcise, and they did not celebrate Passover until the unfaithful generation died off and the new generation was to be sanctified to receive the inheritance.[7]

Passover is far more than a meal shared among God's people. God instituted the Passover as a reminder to celebrate how He rescued the Israelites from terrible bondage in Egypt. Passover is a foretelling of what Jesus' blood, shed on the cross, accomplishes for all believers as the Passover Lamb. The blood-painted doorposts in Egypt were just a picture of what was coming through the Messiah.

Also for the first time in decades, God's people feast on the rich food from the land. Can you imagine how good that tasted after a strict diet of manna for so long?

**Have you ever experienced a time in your life when you went without certain foods or were not able to eat properly? If so, how did it feel to eat "real" food again?**

I remember having strep throat as a child. Swallowing was painful, so I was reduced to soft, cold food. Even though I loved ice cream, it got pretty old after a few days. I still remember how amazing my mom's fried chicken tasted when I was able to swallow without pain once again.

But far beyond food, each day you and I can celebrate God's great deliverance granted to us through Jesus Christ, our Passover Lamb. Through His death and victorious resurrection, we can celebrate each day our freedom from bondage to sin.

The risen power of Christ in us (celebrated in our Baptism and remembered at the Lord's communion table) enables us to triumph over every obstacle and survive any turmoil that the enemy initiates. His living and active power in us brings certain victory. Praise the Lord!

## GO QUIET, GO DEEP

Quiet your mind from distractions and pull your Bible close. Bow your head and ask Jesus to make His Word and today's text personal for you.

Take your time writing out 2 Timothy 3:17.

How has the Lord equipped you over time to serve Him as you do today in a way that you could not have possibly fathomed?

I pray that God continues to keep that sense of wonder alive in you as you serve Him with the special equipping He has given to you.

Lesson 3

# The Fall of Jericho

*(Joshua 5:13–6:27)*

Just as Joshua is about to enter into a life-and-death battle at Jericho, God Himself stands before Joshua outside of the walls of Jericho. He assures Joshua of victory over an intimidating foe in a personal encounter.

We can parallel this with Moses when he faced a life-and-death battle for the freedom of God's people from bondage in Egypt. Then, God assured Moses of His victorious presence. Here, God assures Joshua of His victorious presence. And for you and me, God sent Immanuel, "God with us," to ensure our victory over sin, death, and the grave.

DAY 1: The Commander of the Lord's Army (Joshua 5:13–15)

DAY 2: Instructions for Conquering Jericho (Joshua 6:1–7)

DAY 3: Joshua Instructs the People (Joshua 6:8–14)

DAY 4: Jericho's Walls Come Tumbling Down (Joshua 6:15–25)

DAY 5: The Fall of Jericho (Joshua 6:26–27)

### Key Questions:

- What has been the biggest spiritual battle that you have experienced to date?
- Do you believe that God's presence appears only in places where His people take His Word?
- What victory has God given you that you know without a doubt could not have happened without His direct intervention?

## Day 1

# THE COMMANDER OF THE LORD'S ARMY

*(Joshua 5:13–15)*

Although the following events are contained in only three verses at the end of Joshua 5, a significant page turns as the story of God's people unfolds.

The Israelites are camped across the plain of Moab at Gilgal. The men have recovered from circumcision and are ready to mobilize. A short distance away looms the large, fortified city of Jericho.

### Jericho, the Oldest City in the World

At approximately 10,000 years old, Jericho is the oldest inhabited city archaeologists have discovered since excavations began in the mid-1800s. It is second only to Jerusalem in the order of importance to archaeologists.

I have walked the streets of Jericho. There is an ancient cylindrical tower near the center of the city with a small sign staked in the ground that reads, "The Oldest Structure in the World."

In the center of town, there is a large sign in front of an elaborately tiled water fountain that says, "The Oldest City in the World." A friend took a picture of me sitting on the edge of that fountain in 2010 with that particular sign in the background. Walking through Jericho is truly a remarkable experience.

Located in the middle of the Judean Desert, Jericho is unique in a few key aspects. First, Jericho is an oasis. Literally. Jericho is fed by an underground spring that keeps the city and surrounding farmland well watered and green. Camels romp in nearby fenced enclosures. After traveling through the brown desert barrenness along the Dead Sea, Jericho's lushness is eye candy for every visitor.

How is Jericho referred to in the following verses?

**Deuteronomy 34:3**

**2 Chronicles 28:15**

The city of palm trees must have been a very comfortable place to live in biblical times. Palm trees still dot the landscape today. Interestingly, archaeologists confirmed in the 1930s that a significant destruction of Jericho occurred sometime around 1400 BC. That dateline coincides with the time that Joshua led the Israelites into the Promised Land. Jericho had reached its power during the Middle Bronze Age sometime around 2000 BC, six hundred years before the Israelites arrived. Jericho was an ancient city to be reckoned with.

Jesus will walk through Jericho as well. He heals a blind beggar named Bartimaeus near Jericho (Mark 10:46–52; Luke 18:35–42). And He visits a tax collector named Zacchaeus in Jericho (Luke 19:1–10). In both instances, Jesus opens the gates of heaven to them through faith.

## Joshua Encounters the Preincarnate Christ

**Read Joshua 5:13–14. What stands out to you in these verses?**

Perhaps Joshua is taking a midnight stroll, his mind deep in thought about how to enter and conquer such a fortified city with their simple swords. Israel's new leader gazes upon the walls of Jericho. The Israelites do not possess state-of-the-art battering rams and are inexperienced regarding extended battle sieges. What in the world would his strategy be? As he gazes at Jericho's walls, perhaps Joshua wonders if their weapons would match the challenge. We can only imagine the questions and scenarios that flood Joshua's mind. In the end, the Israelites will enter without having to draw a single sword.

As Joshua reaches Jericho, he lifts his eyes to look up at the city. In that moment, he comes face to face with God Himself.

**How does Joshua 5:13 describe the man standing in front of Joshua?**

**In Joshua 5:14, how does the man identify himself to Joshua?**

Joshua is obviously caught off guard by the appearance of this solitary man holding a drawn sword just outside the city they are about to attack. A sentry? A spy?

**What does Joshua ask the man?**

**What two-letter, one-word answer does the man give?**

Joshua asks a pretty straightforward question. However, the man simply answers *no*. Such an odd answer reveals that Joshua missed the point.

This battle will not be the Israelites against the Canaanites. The real question is whether or not *Joshua* is on *the Lord's* side. The battle is the Lord's, and He has already won it before the Israelites ever approach the walls. In a sense, Israel will be active spectators to the mighty, victorious work of God.

**How does this lend a new perspective to a spiritual battle you may be suiting up for right now?**

**What does Jesus tell us in John 16:33?**

Jesus promises we will face trouble in this world, but He has already won the battle! That does not mean we will not face the enemy. It means that the enemy we face has already been defeated. But we cannot let our guard down. The enemy continues to attack us.

Write out the following verses and keep them handy as you face life's battles:

**1 Corinthians 15:57**

**Exodus 14:14**

**Colossians 2:15**

**How do those verses provide spiritual strength for you in the days and battles to come?**

One question needs to be addressed: How do we know Joshua has encountered the preincarnate Christ and not an angel? The Bible gives us two clues.

**At the end of Joshua 5:14, what does Joshua do?**

Joshua falls on his face and worships the man. As the preincarnate Jesus stands before Joshua, He does not stop Joshua from worshiping Him. Had it been an angel, the angel would have instructed Joshua not to bow in worship (see Revelation 22:9). Instead, Jesus receives Joshua's worship as the only rightful recipient.

There is a second reason we know that Joshua has encountered the preincarnate Christ.

**Read Joshua 5:15. What does the commander of the Lord's army tell Joshua?**

Just as God instructed Moses in Exodus 3:5 through a burning bush, He instructs Joshua to take off his sandals, for the ground on which he walks is holy. The ground is holy because the Lord Himself is present. Joshua has come face to face with the Lord, and he knows it.

The parallel between Moses' and Joshua's encounters with the Lord begs us to ask a question: Does God reveal Himself to us in ways that we need to see Him depending upon our particular circumstances?

Allow me to elaborate. Moses was about to face Pharaoh to demand the release of God's people from Egypt, so God appeared to Moses in a bush that was on fire but did not burn. Moses needed to be encouraged by seeing a miracle-working God.

Joshua is about to square off against one of the most fortified cities in the land of Canaan and claim it for God's people, so God appears to Joshua as a man holding a drawn sword. Joshua needs to be encouraged by seeing God as a warrior ready for battle.

And God reveals Himself to us today through the entirety of His Word. We have the privilege of being encouraged by seeing a death-defeating, resurrection-powerful God.

God is also a personal God who desires an intimate relationship with you. How do you need to see Him today? As a miracle worker? As a victorious warrior? God will not disappoint you because nothing is impossible with Him.

As we close chapter 5, Joshua is kneeling before our mighty God, who commands all of the universe—heaven, the earth, and all that is under the earth—to do His will. As Joshua faces the most formidable city in Canaan, the commander of the Lord's army stands with him.

Regardless of what situation you face this day, this week, or this year, the Commander of the Lord's army stands with you as well.

## GO QUIET, GO DEEP

Quiet your mind from distractions and pull your Bible close. Bow your head and ask Jesus to make His Word and today's text personal for you.

Take your time writing out Psalm 23:4.

What does it mean to you that God is with you?

I pray that God gives you strength and increases your faith as you walk in the truth that He is with you always.

## Day 2

# INSTRUCTIONS FOR CONQUERING JERICHO

*(Joshua 6:1–7)*

Chapter 6 begins a new section in the book of Joshua. Chapters 1–5 dealt with God's people entering the Promised Land. They listened to Joshua as their new God-appointed leader and carefully followed the Lord's instructions through him to the letter.

God has brought them successfully into Canaan, and now it is time to get to work. This chapter begins the epic adventure of God's people conquering the land as their promised inheritance from the Lord.

**Read Joshua 6:1. What stands out to you in the opening verse?**

The people of Jericho are so completely paralyzed by fear that they have completely shut down all traffic entering or exiting the city. No vendors approach and no residents leave. Business as usual comes to an absolute standstill.

The Hebrew word for "shut up" (*sāgar*) indicates that the gates had been shut and fastened with bolts and bars. It is the same word used in Joshua 2:5 when Rahab tells those inquiring about Joshua's two spies that the men had gone out before the city gate was "closed" for the evening.

A city's walls and gates were of paramount importance in biblical times. Such fortified cities kept their residents and belongings safe from marauders by routinely shutting the city's gates at nightfall. Otherwise, the city and its residents were vulnerable to surprise attacks, destruction, or a political coup.

Similarly, in the book of Nehemiah, the Lord sent Nehemiah to rebuild the walls around Jerusalem to secure the city and His people from enemy raids. This explanation provides valuable insight for our study:

> Modern US cities offer little, if any, meaningful comparison, but in Nehemiah's day, a city's wall served as an integral part of its defensive structure. It protected the people, as well as the temple and its priests, whom God used to minister to the people's spiritual needs. In fact, to "possess the gate" of a city was ultimately to control the city itself (Genesis 24:60).[8]

Jericho is on high alert when Joshua and the Israelites reach its gates. God's miracles, performed on behalf of His people, are known far and wide. It does not take a military genius to realize that the Israelites do not approach Jericho to extend an olive branch of peace.

Personally, I do not like violence. So perhaps, like me, you are wondering why God could not simply snap His fingers to remove Israel's enemies and settle them peacefully in the land. And to help us understand, I found this insight helpful:

> Before the rebellion of Satan, war did not exist. . . . Divine warfare is God's means for saving his chosen people. For the sake of [Old Testament] Israel, God engaged in temporal and national warfare, while for the salvation of all believers of both Testaments, God won the spiritual war through the physical death of Jesus on the cross and his bodily resurrection. Without this divine warfare, mankind would have been doomed to eternity in hell, but God's warfare enabled Israel to inherit the promised land, and his victory on the cross has made all believers heirs of eternal life in the new heavens and the new earth.[9]

God fights for us (both then and now) because our enemy will roam back and forth over the earth until Jesus Christ returns. War is a necessary evil in this sin-fallen world.

**In what ways have you seen the evils of warfare (other than physical combat) in our modern day?**

**As a Christ-follower, how can you make a difference in the battle?**

**Read Joshua 6:2–5. Take a moment to write the Lord's words to Joshua in verse 2.**

The verb tense deployed in verse 2 provides a startling revelation. Before Joshua and His people even enter Jericho, God assures Joshua that the battle *has already been won.* God is declaring a future reality as a present promise.

**In Joshua 6:2, what has God promised?**

Not only would the city of Jericho itself fall before Joshua, but so would its king and all the mighty men of valor. Why would that be important for Joshua to know? The answer to that question becomes clear when God lays out the plan of how the city will be taken.

**According to Joshua 6:3–5, with what weapons does God instruct Joshua to "attack" Jericho?**

Now, the Israelites are not military professionals. However, even to them, the strategy might sound absolutely ludicrous. Wars are won or lost by sword and might, not trumpets and marching in a circle. But Joshua does not even flinch. He had seen too much of God's mighty power to laugh at what he had been told. By faith, Joshua believes God will bring them victory exactly as He had instructed.

On a scale of 1 to 10, do you believe that God will bring victory even when you cannot see the way through challenging situations?

NOT CONFIDENT VERY CONFIDENT

1 5 10

Take a moment to write out the following verses about God's faithfulness:

**Philippians 4:6–7**

**Psalm 27:1**

**Hebrews 12:28–29**

God will often exercise tests of faith in our lives. It's not to see us fail but so we can understand our weaknesses and ask God to increase our faith in those areas.

**In James 1:2–4, what is the goal when God tests your faith?**

Standing in front of a well-fortified city with its gates barred presents a significant test of faith for Joshua and the Israelites. They could opt to relax in their tents and continue to take advantage of the delicious food now available in the land while Jericho slowly dies of starvation within its own walls. But Joshua wastes no time in following God's commands.

**Read Joshua 6:6–7. What stands out to you in these verses?**

The number *7* is notably repeated in God's instructions to Joshua. In Lesson 2, Day 3, we touched on the significance of the number *7* regarding the seven nations that the Israelites would conquer.

Seven is considered a meaningful number to God. Following His creation of the world, "God blessed the seventh day and made it holy, because on it God rested from all His work that He had done in creation" (Genesis 2:3). Even though God created the world in six days, the seventh day of rest is counted as an integral part of the creation process.

By repeating the number seven in His instructions to Joshua, God reveals that Jericho's destruction is from God Himself—not because of His people's efforts.

The blasts from seven trumpets will also be an integral part of God's victory over Jericho. As a music lover and a high school band nerd, I love the sound of a trumpet. It is the sound of a call to action. Today's armed forces wake up every morning to a reveille, a call played on a shortened small trumpet called a bugle. Trumpets appear throughout Scripture to signal the presence of God.

On what occasions are trumpets heard and used in the following verses?

**Exodus 19:16–17**

**Exodus 20:18–19**

**Revelation 8:1–2**

Not only do the seven trumpets announce the presence of the Lord, but God instructs Joshua again to carry before them the ark of the covenant. Victory will be theirs!

The area around Jericho is known for earthquakes, and secular scientists readily dismiss the biblical account of how Jericho's walls fell. Just as God used the east wind to part the Red Sea, God could have certainly used earthquakes to bring the walls of Jericho tumbling down.

But that is not what God wants. God wants to show His people that, through faith, seven trumpets blown by seven priests as they march around Jericho seven times are all He needs to deliver the city into their hands.

Through God's assurance to Joshua then and to us today, God provides confidence and comfort that no matter what hardships we face before experiencing victory, we *will* be victorious in Him.

## GO QUIET, GO DEEP

Quiet your mind from distractions and pull your Bible close. Bow your head and ask Jesus to make His Word and today's text personal for you.

Take your time writing out Matthew 19:26.

What does it mean to you that God has given you victory even before your battles begin?

I pray that you take heart that God brings you victory simply because He loves you and desires the best for you.

## Day 3

# JOSHUA INSTRUCTS THE PEOPLE

*(Joshua 6:8–14)*

Yesterday, we studied some very odd instructions that God gave to Joshua about how Jericho would be defeated. Seven trumpets blown by seven priests and followed by the ark of the covenant would march around its walls each day for seven days. And *voilà*! The walls would come tumbling down with a mighty shout.

We can only imagine how strange those instructions sounded to the Israelites. They were likely anticipating hand-to-hand combat with Jericho's inhabitants. I have only seen combat in movies, but I picture battle preparation as armed men sitting around campfires in small groups, sharpening their weapons and discussing strategy. But how this story unfolds is quite different.

**Read Joshua 6:8–11. What stands out to you in these verses?**

As soon as Joshua tells the people God's instructions, they set out to follow what the Lord had commanded without hesitation.

Even though Jericho was an imposing fortified city, archaeologists have discovered that it covered only about half of one square mile. We may envision God's people marching around the city all day and sweating into the night before stumbling back into their camps. However, the whole assembly could have realistically marched around the entire city in about an hour.

God has also instructed the precise order of the people as they march around Jericho.

**According to Joshua 6:9, what was that order?**

The armed men are listed first to lead the assembly. These would have been the advance troops of approximately half a million fighting men. However, they are instructed to use no force. Just march.

Second in line are the seven priests continuously blowing the seven trumpets. The trumpets that the priests would have been blowing are not the shiny brass trumpets that we have today. They are shofars made from rams' horns. Shofars are used in many different ways throughout Scripture.

Take a moment to look up the following verses and write the various ways that shofars were used:

**Leviticus 25:9–10**

**Judges 7:19–21**

**Ezekiel 33:3–6**

**1 Kings 1:34**

**Psalm 98:6**

**1 Thessalonians 4:16–18**

Whether the shofar sounded to gather God's people, proclaim the Year of Jubilee, overcome an enemy, warn of judgment, announce a new king, praise and worship God, or declare the Lord's return, God consistently remains the central focus when a shofar, or trumpet, is blown.

Back to our order of the people. First in line would be the armed men. Second would be the seven priests blowing trumpets. Then, the ark of the covenant, lifted high for all to see, would be in line behind the priests.

**Why do you believe the ark of the covenant is placed in the middle of the assembly instead of leading the charge?**

The ark was usually carried into battle in front of the soldiers at the vanguard of the assault. However, the soldiers in this scenario are commanded not to fight but simply to march.

Consequently, God orders the ark containing the tablets of the Law to be placed in the heart of the marching assembly. Perhaps the Lord realizes that the mere sight of the ark would strengthen the people's courage to continue marching. Placed in the middle, it would be visible to many more.

Even today, it is a faith-strengthener for you and me to have visible reminders of the Lord's central presence in our lives. That reminder may appear as wearing a cross around your neck, hanging a framed Bible passage on your wall, or creating a screensaver with your favorite verse. When we feel anxious or unsure, those visible signs remind us of who is in control.

To complete the order of the marching assembly, the final group is simply referred to as the "rear guard" (Joshua 6:9). Scripture does not specify whether or not the rear guard includes every remaining Israelite. However, considering the size of Jericho compared to the total number of God's people, it is not likely that every person participates. It was not customary for women and children to be part of Old Testament armies.

**In Joshua 6:10, what specific instruction does Joshua give?**

The complete silence of God's people certainly added to the drama of the scene. I mean, how creepy would that be if you were a spectator? But that first day's march is only the first of more to come.

**Read Joshua 6:12–14.**

The second day's march is like the first. Thousands upon thousands of God's people are systematically marching around the circumference of Jericho. The only sounds are their shuffling feet and the eerie blowing of seven shofars. Then it repeats without a change for four more days in a row. Talk about making the hair on the back of your neck stand up for six days straight!

Imagine what the people inside Jericho think as they peek out from the city walls to glimpse the marching horde. Scripture is silent as to their reaction. We know only that they never emerge from Jericho while God's people march around the city.

But for Jericho, those are the sounds of impending doom. The people had lived in unrepentant sin for hundreds of years. God's judgment now slowly encircles them . . . literally.

**According to 1 Timothy 2:4, what is God's desire?**

God's desire is for all people to know Him as their Lord and Savior. Jesus will return to judge the earth only when the Father has determined time is up, so to speak.

That is why a Christian's primary mission is to share the Gospel message without delay. We do not know the day or the hour that Jesus will return (Matthew 24:36), but the clock is ticking. God has given the inhabitants of the land of Canaan more than six centuries to repent and turn toward Him (Genesis 15:16). They have steadfastly refused.

Judgment day has arrived.

## GO QUIET, GO DEEP

Quiet your mind from distractions and pull your Bible close. Bow your head and ask Jesus to make His Word and today's text personal for you.

Take your time writing out 1 Corinthians 1:9.

What does it mean to you that God has called you into fellowship with Jesus Christ?

I pray that the knowledge and truth of God's faithfulness in your life inspires you to be ALL IN as you serve Him.

## Day 4

# JERICHO'S WALLS COME TUMBLING DOWN

*(Joshua 6:15–25)*

For six consecutive days, the Israelites marched around Jericho. There was no change whatsoever to their routine. Each day, they assembled and lined up in the order specified by God. Armed men, seven priests blowing seven trumpets, the ark of the covenant held high in the midst of them, and all followed up by the rear guard.

Then, en masse, they silently circle the city with only the sound of their trumpets and shuffling feet. It is a startling picture of quiet perseverance and steadfast obedience.

This day will be vastly different. The day has finally arrived when the Lord will deliver Jericho, its king, and all its mighty men of valor over to His people.

**Read Joshua 6:15–21. What stands out to you in these verses?**

**According to Joshua 6:15, how many times did God's people march around the city?**

On the seventh consecutive day of marching around the city, God commands that the people march around the city seven times in a row. In our last lesson, we looked at the significance of the number *7* in relationship to God.

We also learned that, considering the size of Jericho, it would have taken God's people roughly an hour to march around the entire city. So, on this seventh day, they spend the better part of the day marching around the city seven times. The tension inside Jericho must be thick, dread growing with every lap. And the anticipation mounting in the hearts of God's people must be palpable too. But before God's people storm into the city, Joshua issues a stern warning.

**Write out what Joshua commands the Israelites in Joshua 6:18–19.**

God deems Jericho to be a *cherem*, a thing devoted to destruction to the Lord. In other words, the people are strictly warned to not take any spoils of war from the city for personal use. All of Jericho's inhabitants are to be destroyed or damned for their wickedness, while the city's treasures, including all money and tangible items, are to be consecrated to the Lord's service in the tabernacle (Joshua 6:24). Not a single gold coin or silver chalice is allowed to be claimed as personal booty.

A natural question to ask is why God would specifically deem Jericho to be a *cherem* when on other occasions in the Bible God allowed people to keep some of the treasure for themselves. I found this explanation helpful:

> [Joshua] 6:19 has implications for the church's stewardship. The church militant wins "victories" as the Gospel advances and God's kingdom expands through the power of his Word and Sacraments. The people and things that are acquired do not belong to the church, its pastors, or its congregations. They belong to the Lord himself, who shed his blood to purchase all sinners and rescue them from eternal destruction. The people and their possessions are "sacred for the Lord" ([Joshua] 6:19). If an Israelite were to take for himself some of the *cherem*, the "things devoted exclusively to the Lord," then he—and the contaminated camp of Israel—would become *cherem*, a "thing damned to destruction" (6:18).[10]

Only by the grace of God does He allow His people, on occasion, to keep His spoils of war. Everything in the heavens, on earth, and under the earth belongs to God alone.

God's command to the Israelites here in Joshua 6 is crystal clear. They are to keep *nothing* of Jericho's spoils and leave *nothing* breathing.

Those are hard words for us to swallow in our modern times. Some may push back and argue that God is mean or unfair to indiscriminately take lives. Some may argue that God certainly took His time pronouncing judgment on the centuries-long sin of the Canaanites.

When evil things happen in this world, we question God about what He is going to do about it. Then, when He does something, we push back and say that it was too "mean."

It is not our job to try to explain God, nor are we to have the temerity to question His almighty actions. God is God, and we are not. But by faith given to us by God, we trust Him no matter what. You and I can be thankful and rest in the ultimate comfort that, because of Jesus' blood, shed for us, we will never experience such wrath from God.

**What does Joshua command the people to do at the end of Joshua 6:16?**

With a mighty sound that must have shaken the very ground beneath their feet, God's people let out a great shout. Can you imagine it? Super Bowl referees with in-ear monitors have trouble hearing over more than 75,000 screaming fans packed into a stadium as the clock ticks down to victory. Now multiply that sound by hundreds of thousands of voices.

Sudden loud sounds such as a car horn or a dog barking unexpectedly make me jump. The residents of Jericho must have jumped straight out of their skin (figuratively speaking) when God's people shouted in one voice.

**As a result of their great shout, what happens to Jericho's wall in Joshua 6:20?**

At long last, the walls of Jericho come tumbling down and God's people storm in to capture the city. What a glorious day! Not only has the Lord delivered Jericho into their hands, but God's people saw another great miracle of Yahweh on their behalf.

**Read Joshua 6:22–25.**

True to his word, Joshua honors the promise that his two spies made to Rahab to ensure that she and her family were rescued before Jericho fell.

**Summarize what happened with Rahab and her family.**

Freedom! Not only are Rahab and her family rescued, but Rahab remains in Israel among God's people, whom she had helped through her bold faith.

**What does Matthew 1:4–5 reveal about Rahab?**

Rahab not only remains in Israel (Joshua 6:25), but she marries an Israelite named Salmon. They have a son named Boaz, who is Ruth's kinsman redeemer. From prostitute to being prominently named in the genealogy of our Lord and Savior Jesus Christ, Rahab is rescued both physically and eternally through faith in God.

**According to Joshua 6:24, what do God's people do to Jericho?**

By its nature, fire renders anything it consumes unrecognizable. But thanks to diligent archaeologists, the collapse of Jericho's walls is not the only interesting biblical fact they have unearthed.

Joshua 5:10–12 reveals that the destruction of Jericho happened during the spring harvest season. Through excavations, archaeologists have uncovered large quantities of harvested grain stored in large containers at Jericho that were burned to a crisp. Such a finding is highly unusual because it was standard practice in biblical times for invaders to gather any food they found for their people before burning a city they conquered.

However, since God had deemed Jericho to be a *cherem*, the Israelites do not remove anything from within its walls (other than treasures dedicated to God) before setting the city on fire. The burned grain discovered in Jericho's containers is yet another instance of science validating the biblical narrative.

Joshua and the Israelites marched around Jericho a total of thirteen times on faith alone. They did not know how God would conquer Jericho, but they trusted God's promise.

Receiving and operating in God's promises takes faith. Faith to believe that God is trustworthy. Faith to keep walking when the path does not make sense. Faith to believe when the situation seems impossible.

One of the main points of the battle of Jericho is that God is the one who will deliver His people. Israel's job is to trust God and wait on His perfect timing. God instructed Joshua to walk around the city and blow trumpets rather than muster men with battering rams.

Jericho's fall is a stunning example of what simple cooperation and meticulous obedience to God can accomplish despite overwhelming odds.

God desires that His people know beyond the shadow of a doubt that every victory we experience wholly and completely depends on Him alone.

## GO QUIET, GO DEEP

Quiet your mind from distractions and pull your Bible close. Bow your head and ask Jesus to make His Word and today's text personal for you.

Take your time writing out Ephesians 3:20–21.

What does it mean to you that God does immeasurably more than can ask or imagine?

I pray that God's faithful love for you empowers you to boldly share His love with others.

## DAY 5

# THE FALL OF JERICHO

*(Joshua 6:26–27)*

Even though the book of Joshua recounts many battles, possessing the land inheritance God promised was the clear objective. Centuries earlier, God had promised the land to Abraham and his descendants. Although conquering the land was important, the spiritual component was of greater importance.

At long last, the city of Jericho and its former inhabitants lie in charred ruins because of their sin. However, as Israel's leader, Joshua has some final words before the Israelites advance further into Canaan.

**Read Joshua 6:26–27. What stands out to you in those verses?**

As Jericho lies in ruins, Joshua's parting words pronounce a curse over the city. This is significant because Jericho is the only conquered city referenced in the Old Testament that received a holy curse.

**What is the curse?**

This curse is twofold. The first part of the curse would strike down the firstborn child of anyone who rebuilt Jericho's foundation. The second part of the curse would strike down the youngest child of anyone who set up the gates (in other words, put the finishing touches on the rebuilt city).

These curses serve as a stern warning to anyone who rebuilds a city that God had destroyed specifically because of its sin. Resurrecting this city that God had condemned would be regarded as an act of evil against the Lord.

These specific curses pronounced by Joshua are carried out during the reign of Ahab and his wife Jezebel.

Read 1 Kings 16:29–34.

**Who lost both his firstborn and youngest son for rebuilding Jericho?**

**What does the last part of 1 Kings 16:34 confirm?**

The curse that Joshua pronounced against Jericho was the word of the Lord, not his own. The Lord does not make idle threats. The abandoned ruins of the destroyed city are intended to serve as a reminder that God judged sin in that place and gave victory to His people. Hiel of Bethel did not heed the Lord's warning at the cost of two of his children.

Curses were common in ancient times. However, people regarded them as magical mumbo jumbo unless there were actual consequences. But the Lord's curses were specifically pronounced as a penalty for not obeying His Law. The judgment was very real.

You and I will feel the consequences of our sins too. For example, when we lose our temper with a loved one, we will feel the consequences of losing the affection and trust of that person for a while. However, God does not judge our actions as unforgivable transgressions against Him. Our merciful God provided His Son to absorb His holy judgment for all of our sins—past, present, and future.

**Write out 1 Peter 2:24.**

**God absorbed our sin in the body of His one and only Son. What is your response to such love?**

Many people say that they have a list of questions for Jesus when they get to heaven. I don't know about you, but I believe my knees will not be able to hold me up once I see Him face to face. Face-down worship is far more likely than a face-to-face interview.

God's people now inhabit the Promised Land and conquer their first city. For Israel to inherit the land God promised, their lives and hearts need to stand in a right spiritual relationship with the God who loves and guides them.

Observing, worshiping, and obeying God needs to remain at the center of the Israelites' new life in the Promised Land. They are now surrounded by pagan cultures that could easily lead them astray.

In our modern culture, you and I are surrounded by corruption, greed, lust, power grabs, political dishonesty, border invasions, and wars in various parts of the world (to name a few threats).

**In our pagan culture today, how do you intentionally keep God at the center of your life?**

Encouraging fellow Christians as they stand on the spiritual battlefield is a huge part of that intentionality. What do the following verses say about that?

**1 Thessalonians 5:11**

**Hebrews 3:13**

Encouraging each other along the journey is vital. God has been faithful and gracious to surround us with a great cloud of witnesses (Hebrews 12:1–2) who have gone before us and who labor alongside us. Supporting each other through prayer and service is a great privilege and faith booster.

Archaeologists have been able to confirm a substantial amount of information provided in the book of Joshua. They discovered that the entire culture of some Canaanite cities dramatically changed over five specific years during the time God's people settled in Canaan.

For instance, they uncovered evidence (building styles and pottery fragments) that between 1250 and 1200 BC the inhabitants of cities such as Lachish, Hazor, and Bethel embraced a far simpler lifestyle. Those dates and changes specifically coincide with how those cities were conquered according to the book of Joshua.

As one who has downsized significantly in the past few years and moved into full-time writing and teaching ministry, a simpler life frees my time and resources for the Lord.

**According to Joshua 6:27, what does God do for Joshua?**

Joshua could not take a bunch of ex-slaves with no military training into a well fortified city and flatten its walls. Even though Jericho's destruction was His work, God allows the limelight to fall upon Israel's leader. Mankind often needs to see an earthly example of godly leadership.

**If the Lord has placed a godly leader whom you greatly admire in an area of your life, how do you see the fingerprints of God in that leader's life?**

If that leader is still living, consider sending him or her a note of encouragement and thanks while it is still today. It is inspiring to see godly leaders wholeheartedly following the Lord and being blessed by the Lord for their faithfulness. It also inspires us to search the Bible to discover what other characteristics the Lord greatly esteems that we could emulate on our spiritual journey.

The book of Joshua is not merely a history of Israel. Rather, it contains the history of what the God of Israel did for His people.

God, our living God, is active in time and history to work on behalf of His people. He faithfully brought about what He promised to Joshua in biblical times, and He will do the same for you and me in modern times.

God deserves *all* the glory.

## GO QUIET, GO DEEP

Quiet your mind from distractions and pull your Bible close. Bow your head and ask Jesus to make His Word and today's text personal for you.

Take your time writing out Psalm 119:93.

What does it mean to you that God's precepts (teachings) have given you life?

I pray that you work diligently to remember God's precepts and live out your days with a sense of constant wonder at how much He loves you.

## LESSON 4

# THE COST OF BROKEN FAITH

*(Joshua 7–8)*

As we studied Joshua 6, we saw God's people filled with faith and hope as God brought miraculous victories to them. They wholeheartedly trusted God and followed Joshua into battle to conquer the city of Jericho.

Joshua 7 stands in stark contrast. The dark underbelly of rebellion rears its ugly head in the form of covenant-breaking greed and grief caused by sin.

Faithful to His Word, God does not leave them defeated and does not cast out the Israelites from His presence. He encourages and equips His people to become victors instead of victims.

DAY 1: Israel's First Defeat in Canaan (Joshua 7:1–9)

DAY 2: Hidden Sin Uncovered (Joshua 7:10–26)

DAY 3: Joshua Prepares to Battle Ai (Joshua 8:1–9)

DAY 4: The Fall of Ai (Joshua 8:10–29)

DAY 5: Joshua Renews the Covenant (Joshua 8:30–35)

### KEY QUESTIONS:

- Have you ever thought a particular sin in your life was so bad that it outstripped God's forgiveness and love?
- How did God reassure you of His faithfulness and encourage you to repent and return to Him?
- After that time, how did you renew your commitment to God?

## DAY 1

# ISRAEL'S FIRST DEFEAT IN CANAAN

*(Joshua 7:1–9)*

Working as a team was integral to my high school's "Mighty Eagle" marching band. Our band director grouped us by instrument sections to form squads during summer band practice. Each squad was led by an upperclassman who was assigned to teach the squad the routine that he or she had already learned.

After a particularly frustrating session one scorching August day, one of the members of my squad decided to give back talk our squad leader. The result was that the whole squad had to march in place for two minutes as punishment. As you can imagine, we made sure that our mouthy squad member felt our resentment, and it never happened again.

Up to this point, God's people have walked in faithful obedience, unlike their parents who were buried in the desert. But that obedience disappears in a flash with one man's greedy actions.

**Read Joshua 7:1.**

After such obedience and faithfulness to God's commands to defeat Jericho, this is a sad opening sentence to chapter 7.

Achan takes from Jericho some of the things devoted to destruction and hides them. And even though only one man disobeyed God, all of Israel would be held accountable.

How is God described in the following verses?

**Hebrews 12:29**

**Deuteronomy 9:3**

Although God's anger was usually aroused when His people worshiped other gods, the fire of God's anger burns consistently against the enemies of His people. However, in Joshua 7:1, the flames of the Lord's anger are aimed straight at the Israelites.

More often than not, the effects of one person's sinful actions spill over into the lives of others. (Thank you, Adam and Eve.) We can easily relate to that principle even today. For instance, when a person chooses to drink and then get behind the wheel of a car, the resulting ramifications can be devastating to the family and friends of the victims injured or killed (as well as those of the driver).

All of us can likely remember something we said, did, or hid that adversely affected others. Every generation struggles with sin. The same that was true for the Israelites is true for us. Sometimes we have enemies that come at us from the outside, but our greatest enemy comes from our sinful nature inside us.

Achan breaks faith and all the Israelites suffer. The phrase "broke faith" in Joshua 7:1 refers to willful acts of unfaithfulness against the Lord's commands. To state it bluntly, Achan has a much bigger problem than worrying whether or not his fellow Israelites would discover his thievery. God knows. And you cannot hide anything from God.

The Israelites had been wandering the wilderness for forty years before entering the Promised Land. They had not enjoyed the normal comforts of daily life in a very long time. Imagine the Israelites feasting their eyes on the city after storming over the fallen walls of Jericho. Proper beds, perhaps running water, even toilets. One wonders if part of the Israelites' test of faith is if they could wait on the Lord's blessings given in the Lord's time rather than when the random opportunity presents itself.

By definition, temptation is an enticement to act in disobedience to God's will. In simple terms, temptation is a test where we are given the choice of being faithful or unfaithful to God.

**What is the last temptation you struggled through? What happened?**

If you struggle with temptation, take a moment to write out the following verses that will help you remain faithful to God:

**1 Corinthians 10:13**

**James 4:7**

Oftentimes, the euphoria of victory makes us more vulnerable to temptation. And the crash of resulting sin can be devastating personally, relationally, and throughout the church. Keeping our eyes on the Lord and remaining vigilant is crucial.

**Read Joshua 7:2–5.**

Unaware of Achan's sin, Joshua sends men to spy on Ai as the Israelites prepare to attack it. The soldiers literally went up, since Jericho sat eight hundred feet below sea level and Ai was located on the mountain ridge that runs through the center of the land (known as the "spine of Israel").

**What do the soldiers report back to Joshua?**

After soundly defeating Jericho with its fortified ramparts, they are lulled into a false sense of security (both in the number of men needed and the lack of knowledge regarding Achan's sin). Joshua issues the order for the soldiers to attack Ai. As a result, the Israelites suffer a devastating, unexpected defeat. The Israelites are not only attacked from the rear as they try to retreat from the battle, but they also lost thirty-six fighting men.

**At the end of verse 5, what is the response of God's people?**

Earlier, when the Israelites drew near to Jericho, the Canaanite hearts melted in fear. Here, it is the hearts of God's people that melt in fear and discouragement.

Perhaps they believed that as long as God was with them, they would never face defeat. After all, the walls of Jericho came crashing down with one mighty shout from His people. There is nothing like defeat in battle and loss of life to bring the reality of war crashing back in.

Whereas the battle of Jericho showed God's faithfulness, the battle of Ai shows Israel's failure. The contrasting battles of Jericho and Ai make a very clear point: If Israel is going to successfully conquer the land of their inheritance, they must be obedient to God and trust His commands.

**Read Joshua 7:6–9. As Joshua and the elders learn of their resounding defeat, what is their first response?**

It was common practice in biblical times to demonstrate signs of grief outwardly, such as tearing clothes and wearing sackcloth and ashes. Mordecai did it when Haman decreed the genocide of the Persian Jews (Esther 4:1). Job did it when he lost his family and possessions (Job 1:20). Joshua and the elders also express outward signs of grief at the news of their first battle loss.

Joshua had been completely unaware of what Achan had done. He could have chosen to shake his fist at heaven and blame God. Yet, Joshua again displays humble faith. Even though he does not understand what happened and why they experienced defeated, his first response is to seek understanding from the Lord who sees all.

**When situations do not turn out as you planned, what is your first reaction?**

Joshua's wise response to seek understanding from the Lord instead of lay blame teaches us much. When we do not understand what is happening around us or to us, our first response needs to be to put our face in the dust and seek God. It is better to come to God with our honest emotions and questions than to not come to God at all.

**When was the last time you went face down (literally or as a posture of your spirit) before the Lord when confusing circumstances blindsided you?**

Many confusing circumstances and blatantly godless actions surround us in our modern tumultuous times. Here are some powerful Scripture passages to write out and use in your prayer time as you seek the Lord's wisdom:

**Proverbs 18:10**

**Romans 5:3–5**

**Romans 8:25–27**

Rather than questioning God about the circumstances from a stance of pride and rebellion, Joshua questions God from a stance of humility and brokenness. Joshua's brokenness, reverence, and honesty before the Lord are inspiring and convicting.

**What question does Joshua ask the Lord at the end of Joshua 7:9?**

The punctuation to Joshua's questions is the glory of God. Joshua shows concern about God's great name, not about his own reputation as Israel's leader. What a beautiful leadership example to follow. His response is reminiscent of Moses' response to God after His people formed a golden calf in Exodus 32:11–14.

When we intentionally sin, are we more convicted and broken about how bad it reflects on God's great name or ours? Joshua and Moses were completely convinced that their lives, ministries, and reputations were set apart to exalt the glory of God.

May the same be said of this generation.

## GO QUIET, GO DEEP

Quiet your mind from distractions and pull your Bible close. Bow your head and ask Jesus to make His Word and today's text personal for you.

Take your time writing out Proverbs 11:2.

What does it mean to you to be humble before the Lord?

I pray that in those moments when you fall into sin, you humble yourself before the Lord. He will faithfully lift you up once again.

## Day 2

# HIDDEN SIN UNCOVERED

*(Joshua 7:10–26)*

When I was in high school, our band took a two-day trip to the Six Flags amusement park in Dallas, Texas. In exchange for free entrance tickets, our band was asked to play a short concert in the park for the visitors each day. Once our job was done, our band chaperones released us to play in the park for the rest of the day. We had an incredible time riding every ride, eating junk food, and getting sunburned.

After the allotted time on our final day in the park, we met back at the buses, ready to depart for the four-hour ride back to Houston. But we didn't depart—we stayed. We grew restless as we sat on the buses for a very long time.

It turned out that two of our band members had been caught shoplifting in one of the park's merchandise stores. The park police were holding them in the administrative offices until the band chaperones could reach their parents to determine what would happen next.

I was devastated when I found out the students caught shoplifting were very good friends of mine. We had known each other for years and often spent time hanging out together and doing fun activities apart from school functions. All our parents knew each other. Somehow, it felt like they had betrayed the foundational trust of our friendship even though their actions had nothing to do with me.

Since they were underage and they returned what they had stolen, no formal charges were filed with the authorities. Their parents had to drive to Dallas to pick them up (the rest of us could only imagine what that ride home must have been like). The two students were also banned from all extracurricular band functions for the rest of the year, including playing at school sports matches and pep rallies.

Today's lesson deals with theft and consequences much more dramatic than a slap on the wrist. Before the Israelites even entered Jericho, God made it crystal clear that His people were to take nothing from the city as spoils of war (Joshua 6:17–19). Yet, a man named Achan willfully disregards God's command and takes some of the devoted things anyway. He not only betrays his family, friends, and fellow soldiers, but he betrays God.

**Read Joshua 7:10–15. Summarize how the Lord responds to Joshua's mourning.**

As believers, there is a time for falling on our face before the Lord and then there is a time for action. God quickly reminds Joshua that this is a moment of action.

We can easily get in the habit of praying, praying, and praying but never moving forward. Once Joshua finishes praying, God instructs him to get up and immediately address the sin that Achan committed.

**Why do you believe it is important to deal with sin without delay?**

The longer you and I wait to "face the music" of our sin, the more time we have to try and justify our actions or downplay the spiritual consequences.

Even though sin may be in our own tent, it can affect the whole camp. Achan's sin and God's reaction to it provide three helpful insights.

**What does Paul tell us in 1 Corinthians 5:9–13?**

First, sin forfeits God's favor. We cannot hold on to sin with one hand and cherish God in the other.

**What does God tell Joshua in Joshua 7:12?**

Second, sin weakens our ability to fight. We cannot slam dunk the tasks God has given us if we stubbornly sit with sin.

**What does God tell Joshua in Joshua 7:13?**

Third, sin separates us from God. The sooner we repent and turn from it, the sooner God will restore our relationship with Him.

**How have you seen this truth play out in your life?**

Repentance and turning from sin are hard, but all things are possible with God.

**Read Joshua 7:16–21.**

God affords the Israelites a chance to get rid of sin and live wholly in His blessing and power. So God tells Joshua to deal with the sin in the camp without delay. In response, Joshua begins a tribe-by-tribe, clan-by-clan, and man-by-man search to find the guilty party whose sin had caused their defeat at Ai.

After an exhaustive, time consuming search, Achan finally confesses. Achan did not come forward to confess and repent. Instead, like a child caught with his hand in the cookie jar, he hid and had to be found. In Achan's confession, he provides the key to how that particular sin came into his life: "*I saw.*" The whole mess came down to where Achan's eyes had wandered.

We cannot miss the gravity of that moment when applied to our own lives. When we think of the catastrophic consequences of sin in our own lives or the lives of those we know or admire, it almost always comes back to where our eyes wander.

How do you see that truth in the following scenarios?

**Genesis 3:6–7**

**2 Samuel 11:1–4**

Both Eve and King David *saw* and then dove headlong into sin. The look is the hook and arouses the flesh. Looking becomes desire, and desire becomes action. Where our eyes linger matters. And the devil is a student of our behavior. He and his minions notice where our eyes linger and prepare tempting fruit to dangle before us accordingly.

The truth is that, given the right circumstances, any of us could be Achan. At face value, he seems to be a normal, intelligent Israelite—at least smart enough to coordinate the secret theft of some of the spoils of war. He belongs to the tribe of Judah, who was always in the thick of fighting Israel's enemies. He is not singled out as strange or corrupt but as a person who could not resist temptation.

There are always consequences for sin.

**Read Joshua 7:22–26. What stands out to you in these verses?**

Achan and his family pay the ultimate price for his greed-driven sin. Even though Achan is stoned to death for his sin, that does not mean he was relegated to hell. It is similar to the thief on the cross next to Jesus who defends Jesus to the other thief and asks Jesus to remember him. Even though that thief dies for his sin, Jesus promises that he will be with Jesus in paradise.

> Repentant believers who are taken from death row to their execution by civil justice are ushered into paradise ([Luke] 23:43). Faith in the saving Lord may have been present in Achan at the time of his honest confession and just execution.[11]

Achan knew he had sinned because he tried to hide the stolen things. His greed has brought fear into the hearts of God's people and cost the lives of thirty-six Israelites, plus himself and his family. Consequently, the place where they are buried is aptly named the Valley of Achor, which means "valley of trouble." Ironically, the likely location of this valley is not far from Jericho, where the Israelites experienced a great triumph.

All the suffering caused by Achan's sin proves that no one is an island. Deliberate disobedience to the will and purpose of God always carries consequences and ripple effects that are far more serious than we can imagine.

God's stance against sin is immovable, but He still invites sinful people into a relationship with Him despite failures. Godly sorrow that leads to repentance is the key to restoring intimacy with God. God delights in being merciful (Micah 7:18).

Even though we have all sinned and fallen short of the glory of God (Romans 3:23), we leave today's session with these beautiful words from 1 John 1:9: "If we confess our sins, He is faithful and just to forgive us our sins and to cleanse us from all unrighteousness."

Thank You, Jesus.

## GO QUIET, GO DEEP

Quiet your mind from distractions and pull your Bible close. Bow your head and ask Jesus to make His Word and today's text personal for you.

Take your time writing out Proverbs 4:25–27.

What does it mean to you to keep your eyes on an upright, moral path?

I pray that God provides for you the daily strength to keep your eyes pure and focused on Him rather than the things of this world.

## DAY 3

# JOSHUA PREPARES TO BATTLE AI

*(Joshua 8:1–9)*

One particularly hot summer's day when I was about twelve years old, my sisters and I decided to sneak into our neighbor's backyard to swim in their pool without adult supervision. Our parents were at work and the pool's owners were on vacation, so we took full advantage of the situation.

My high-school-age older sister had been left in charge of us, but my younger sisters and I cajoled and prodded her. "*It's so hot, think of how good that water will feel. We're supposed to have fun on summer break! We're good swimmers, c'mon!*" She caved. We decided to get into the neighbor's backyard by doing a catwalk along the top of their tall wooden fence to bypass the locked gate. The alert stay-at-home moms on the block saw our fence-top parade (we would have made terrible burglars), realized where we were headed, and called our parents at work. Not long after we had jumped into the pool in reckless summer abandon, we looked up to see several stern-looking neighborhood parents—including our own—staring down at us.

I cannot remember my parents ever being angrier at us than they were that day. Looking back, I realize that their anger stemmed from the heart-stopping fear that their four daughters could have drowned. It was the only time I remember receiving a spanking from my dad (and it was a half-hearted effort at best). Then my mom stood us in four separate corners in a time-out and grounded us from fun summertime activities for two weeks.

After my sisters and I were released from time-out that day, I vividly remember how much I struggled to look my parents in the eyes. I felt so ashamed that I had disobeyed them and caused them such unnecessary fear for my safety. I did not feel that I deserved their love or trust after that. My response stemmed in part from the hormonal drama of female adolescence; my parents' love for us never wavered, and life continued accordingly.

When you and I sin, we may not feel like we have the right to seek God's face ever again. As if somehow our actions have permanently damaged our relationship with Him. Nothing could be further from the truth. The Israelites were about to experience God's redeeming work in their lives once again.

**Read Joshua 8:1–2.**

After the discouraging and horrifying events of chapter 7, it is time for God to rally Joshua and His people to remind them of His faithfulness. Joshua 8 begins with God encouraging Joshua and His people despite Achan's sinful failure.

Rather than letting Israel linger in discouragement and shame over Achan's actions, God speaks encouragement to Joshua and His people.

**In Joshua 8:1, what are God's first words to Joshua?**

True to Joshua 1:6, Joshua had been strong and courageous to root out and deal with Achan's sin. So Joshua reminds God's people that God is still with them and will continue to bring victory to His people.

**Write out 1 John 4:16–19.**

**What comfort do you find in this passage?**

God has not given us a spirit of fear but of power and love and a sound mind (2 Timothy 1:7). God desires for us to be in a relationship with Him, not cower in fear. So God's first words to Joshua remind him not to give in to the discouragement of fear.

**In Joshua 8:2, what does God promise Joshua?**

As with Jericho, God has already given them victory over Ai before the battle even begins. However, God instructs Joshua to take *all* the fighting men with him into battle.

**How does this contrast with how Joshua originally approached Ai in Joshua 7:2–3?**

In stark contrast to Jericho, God's people are permitted to plunder the city and keep all the spoils of war for themselves. Perhaps this was God's way of rewarding their faithfulness (except for Achan) for obeying His command to surrender all of Jericho's spoils to the Lord's treasury.

**Read Joshua 8:3–9. What similarities and differences do you notice between this battle and Jericho?**

Joshua gathers thirty thousand fighting men (ten times more than the failed attack of Ai) to impart the instructions of the Lord. Rather than marching around Ai like at Jericho, God commands them to ambush the city instead.

Joshua's real-time military experience surfaces for the first time since entering the Promised Land. Ambush is a unique tactic of war requiring a higher skill set than mere muscle. A successful ambush of an enemy requires accurate knowledge of the layout of the land, precise assessment of the enemy's location, and detailed information regarding how to gain access to the heart of the enemy's camp. This siege would be much harder than simply climbing over fortified walls already knocked down by the Lord.

**What does God promise in Joshua 8:7?**

Like He had done at Jericho, God has already promised victory to His people before they even begin the battle. This scenario reminds me of Jesus' work on the cross on our behalf. Before we begin each day, Jesus has already won the victory for us over sin and death. In fact, He won the battle for us before we even knew there was a battle on our horizon.

**Write out 1 Corinthians 15:54–57.**

Our enemy is constantly scheming and plotting against us. We cannot be part-time Christians when we have a full-time enemy. Jesus goes before us, and, by faith, we follow where He leads.

**In Joshua 8:8, what does Joshua command the people to do to the city?**

God decrees that the city, like Jericho, shall be burned. The reason is that Ai and all its people have been devoted to destruction, "according to the Word of the Lord."

> This is an example of God's judgment and sentence against all sin and sinners. Thanks be to God, He judges us "not guilty" in Christ.[12]

Almost two entire chapters of the book of Joshua are devoted to the story of Ai.

**Besides Ai, what city is mentioned in Joshua 8:9?**

Bethel held great significance in the role of two of the patriarchs. After God called Abraham to pull up stakes to follow Him, Abram built an altar to the Lord between Bethel and Ai on his way to Egypt in order to call on the name of the Lord (Genesis 12:8). Later, when Jacob was fleeing from Esau, Jacob had a vivid dream about the angels of God ascending and descending on a ladder between heaven and earth (Genesis 28:10–19). The next morning, Jacob took the stone that he had used as a pillow, stood it up (like an ebenezer), and poured oil on it to commemorate the Lord's presence.

Consequently, the place between Ai and Bethel where Joshua and thirty thousand of God's mighty men of valor are waiting to ambush the city is a place God knew intimately because of Abraham. This also reminds me of the Lord's presence with Rahab long before Jericho's walls came tumbling down.

God always goes before His people. When we keep faithful eyes on Him, God will faithfully bring victory to us even in our failed places. Only God can bring victory where we have experienced defeat.

So what happened to my friends who stole from Six Flags? They returned the stolen items and apologized to the park officials and the entire band. God set their feet back on the right path. One of them graduated from high school with honors and we remain friends to this day.

What a beautiful reminder that redemption awaits all who turn their eyes to the Lord through faith.

## GO QUIET, GO DEEP

Quiet your mind from distractions and pull your Bible close. Bow your head and ask Jesus to make His Word and today's text personal for you.

Take your time writing out 1 John 1:9.

What does it mean to you to confess your sins and receive God's forgiveness?

I pray that you relentlessly confess any and all sin to the Lord so that He restores you into fellowship with Him and the Body of Christ.

## Day 4

# THE FALL OF AI

*(Joshua 8:10–29)*

The day of Ai's second battle has arrived. The preceding session revealed that God commanded Joshua to again fight Ai. But this time the Israelites have one important advantage: God has already given them victory.

After dealing with Achan's sin that had caused Israel's first defeat, Joshua again rises early, stirs the people, and approaches Ai.

**Read Joshua 8:10–17. What stands out to you in these verses?**

The author takes care to note that the elders go with Joshua (along with the mighty men of valor) before the battle begins.

**Why would such a detail be important?**

The elders' presence signals their faithfulness to Joshua as God's chosen leader, much like in our churches today, where our elders and lay leaders walk alongside pastors in unity of purpose to do God's will.

Now, this prebattle scene contains many interesting geographical details. Joshua and the men encamp in full view of Ai on its north side. However, they strategically situate themselves where a ravine lies between them and the city. Such a position makes it difficult for Ai to execute a surprise attack on the Israelite army.

To prepare for the ambush, Joshua extracts five thousand fighting men as a rear guard. He hides them out of view of the city's entrance in a valley on the west side of the city. Then, with the troops in place, the army spends the night in the valley.

When the king of Ai notices the huge contingent of soldiers camped just outside his city, he marshals his soldiers and attacks Joshua's large encampment of soldiers that is in full view. Israel feigns defeat and begins a haphazard mock retreat. Consequently, the king calls all of Ai's people to pursue Joshua's soldiers, leaving his city gates wide open. The phrase "hindsight is twenty-twenty" comes to mind here.

**In Joshua 8:17, who joins the fight on Ai's side?**

Scholars believe that there may have been a treaty between Bethel and Ai to help defend each other's cities should the need arise. By the time Joshua entered the Promised Land, Canaan was comprised of several independent city-states rather than a few large cities (like Jericho). A common enemy often led those smaller city-states to combine forces.

**Read Joshua 8:18–23. Why do you think God has Joshua hold a javelin?**

Ambushes require silent, powerful symbols to order attacks. Joshua does not issue a loud war cry or sound a trumpet. Instead, he raises a javelin. Here, we see a parallel to Moses holding up his hands as Israel defeated Amalek.

**Read Exodus 17:10–13. What stands out to you in these verses?**

Joshua was an integral part of that battle with Moses as well. He witnessed firsthand that God gave His people victory as long as Moses held up his hands. And Joshua never forgot.

**Read Joshua 8:24–29. What does Joshua 8:26 reveal?**

Joshua brandishes the javelin until the Lord brings complete victory as He had promised. Joshua is the picture of faithful obedience as he holds the javelin high. I found this insight helpful:

> Joshua's outstretched hand with his javelin is the spiritual symbol that triggers the ambush force into physical action. If the distance involved was not too great, those in the ambush force could see with their own eyes the raised javelin. . . .Joshua holds the position that the great Moses once held. He deserves the respect and obedience once given Moses. The LORD is continuing to exalt Joshua in the eyes of Israel ([Joshua] 3:7; 4:14).[13]

As I pictured Joshua holding the javelin high, I instantly thought of prayer. Sometimes, the weight and depth of our prayers make us weary. But God encourages us through His Word that nothing is impossible with Him. He will bring about the perfect results according to His perfect will and in His perfect timing.

As he did in Jericho, Joshua puts to death all the inhabitants of Ai because God had devoted them to destruction, including its king. The smoke rising from the city signals the remainder of the Israelite's larger force to return from their mock withdrawal.

**According to Joshua 8:29, what is the fate of Ai's king?**

Even though those are hard words to read, such action toward a conquered city's king was the usual practice in biblical times. They did not leave the king hanging past sunset because, according to Mosaic Law, God's people were prohibited from leaving a body hanging overnight: "his body shall not remain all night on the tree, but you shall bury him the same day, for a hanged man is cursed by God" (Deuteronomy 21:23).

Also, we see here again that a heap of stones is raised over someone who was disobedient to the Lord. Achan had sinned against God by taking some of the devoted things. He was stoned to death and stones piled over his body. The King of Ai was part of the Canaanite enemy who had never been on God's side. Upon his death, stones are piled over his body.

**What difference do you see between where the heaps of stones were raised over Achan's body (Joshua 7:26) and the king's body (Joshua 8:29)?**

In Achan's case, perhaps the stones piled in the valley served as a reminder of where one of God's own had sinned. In the king's case, perhaps the stones piled at Ai's main entrance serve as a reminder of the fate that awaits all who do not turn to the Lord.

In both cases, the stones remind people that God brought about overwhelming victory for those who obeyed Him. By the grace of God, those who believe in Christ as their Lord and Savior receive forgiveness and new life.

Write out the following verses that affirm that soul-freeing truth:

**1 John 1:9**

**Ephesians 1:7**

**Isaiah 55:7**

As we close out this saga involving the city of Ai, we leave its pages with two piles of stones. The first pile of stones stands as a reminder of the importance of following God's commands. The second stands as a reminder to God's people then and now that God brings victory for all who obey Him.

Our Rock of Ages is faithful!

## GO QUIET, GO DEEP

Quiet your mind from distractions and pull your Bible close. Bow your head and ask Jesus to make His Word and today's text personal for you.

Take your time writing out Psalm 20:6–7.

What does it mean to you that God brings you victory in life's battles?

I pray that you continue to put your faith in the Lord rather than in the things of this world to win your battles.

## Day 5

# JOSHUA RENEWS THE COVENANT

*(Joshua 8:30–35)*

Joshua and the Israelites are quickly becoming seasoned warriors. To date, they have battled against two significant Canaanite cities. Jericho was defeated by a mighty shout of God's people as God laid down its walls. And Ai was defeated in the Israelites' first armed combat victory.

Now the time has come to rest and celebrate what the Lord has done for them. So Joshua gathers God's people at Mount Ebal.

**Read Joshua 8:30–35. What stands out to you in those verses?**

The narrow valley of Shechem provides lovely serenity flanked by two shade-giving mountains: Ebal and Gerizim. It is said to be one of the most beautiful locations in Palestine. The topography forms a natural amphitheater where a great multitude of people can be addressed and easily hear the one speaking.

Now, in chapter 8, after centuries of misery and anguish, the Israelites experience victory and a respite of peace in the land of their inheritance. This tranquil setting on Mount Ebal is where Joshua gathers God's people.

**In Joshua 8:30, what is the first thing Joshua does?**

Our modern-day understanding of celebration involves much noise, flag-waving, laughter, food, and drink. Just think back to the last birthday party you attended.

In biblical times, celebration usually involved some sort of parade or sumptuous banquet. However, Joshua chooses to celebrate the God who brought them victory by renewing their covenant. And his first order of business is to build an altar to the Lord.

Building an altar symbolizes and solidifies their claim to the land that God had promised them through their forefathers.

**Read Deuteronomy 11:26–30. What stands out to you in these verses?**

Joshua is simply carrying out the very things that Moses had commanded before they even crossed into the Promised Land. The Lord's command through Moses had not changed or expired. Joshua is faithfully keeping God's people faithful to God's Law.

There is an important truth to emphasize in light of Joshua's actions: God's Word never changes. He is the same yesterday and today and forever (Hebrews 13:8). His commands given to us through His Word have not expired.

What does God command in the following verses?

**Matthew 22:37**

**John 13:34–35**

**Colossians 3:13**

Those commands are easy to read, but it takes faith, strength, and the grace of God for us to keep them. It is hard to love the difficult. It is hard to forgive the betrayer. But what a celebration when God brings us victory over those hard situations!

Then, of course, there are the actual Ten Commandments. They have never changed since God gave them to Moses. Unlike the laws that govern our country, amendments to the Commandments do not exist. This brings up a relevant point in our text.

**In Joshua 8:32, what does Joshua do?**

After such a miraculous entrance into the Promised Land and two momentous victories, the Israelites need to be reminded of what God has commanded for those who love Him and are called according to His purpose.

When was the last time you read the Ten Commandments from Scripture? Let's take time now to recite what Moses wrote and what Joshua now copies.

**Read Exodus 20:3–17 aloud.**

Now that you have just read them aloud, try to recite them from memory in any order. Did you forget one or two? If so, which one(s)?

I forgot the "carved image" commandment just now. I did not forget it because I believe it is unimportant. Rather, I simply cannot begin to imagine carving any kind of recognizable image in the first place, much less bowing down to worship it. Like you and me, the Israelites need to be reminded of God's Law. Only then can God's people begin to grasp the indescribable grace and mercy that God pours into our lives daily.

Speaking of carved images, Joshua 8:31 specifically points out that the stones used to build Joshua's altar to the Lord must be uncut stones "upon which no man had wielded an iron tool." Why would God be so specific? I found this explanation helpful:

> Why no iron tools? Part of the answer probably is that such tools could be used to make idolatrous images on the stones in violation of the First Commandment. . . . Natural stones would

> also help keep the altar itself from being venerated as an idol. Another part of the answer may be that iron was associated with swords and war. . . . [Joshua] 8:30–35 represents a time of peace.[14]

This may seem an odd command, but take a moment to think about the centuries-old historic cathedrals that still stand around the world today. Those cathedrals feature gilded carvings, marble altars, and precious wood, and it almost seems like the builders competed to out-decorate each other's architectural works of art. Here, God basically says that less is more.

### Mountains of Blessings and Curses

Joshua has fulfilled two of the three parts listed by Moses in Deuteronomy 11:26–30: build an altar and copy the words of the Law on large stones.

**According to Joshua 8:33, what do they do next?**

Can you imagine that scene? The Valley of Shechem was narrow, so Joshua divides the people into two groups with the ark of the covenant between them. Just as Moses commanded in Deuteronomy 27–28, the people facing Mount Gerizim to the south pronounce blessings while the people facing Mount Ebal to the north pronounce curses.

These blessings and curses followed the old covenant that promised blessings for all who are obedient to God's Law and curses for all who are not.

**According to Deuteronomy 27:15–26, which kinds of acts are cursed by God?**

**According to Deuteronomy 28:1–14, what are some of the blessings of God?**

Those are some weighty curses and incredible blessings! As Joshua gathers the Israelites before those mountains, it is clear that honoring God through renewing the covenant is the central focus.

The book of Joshua often emphasizes the presence of the ark of the covenant. The same holds true here when Joshua and the people hold their covenant renewal ceremony. The ark is a symbol of God's presence. The covenant represents His relationship with His people.

As they stand at the foot of the mountains, Joshua reads the entirety of all that Moses had commanded. Hearing those words ringing between the rock faces in the natural amphitheater of Shechem must have been extraordinary.

Before we wrap up this day's session, there is an important nuance that needs to be highlighted so that we do not miss it.

**In Joshua 8:35, who is included in the covenant renewal?**

God does not leave out any faithful believer—whether native-born or sojourner. To use New Testament vocabulary, God's covenant is valid for both the Jew and the Gentile.

Jesus initially tells His disciples to share the Gospel only with Jews who He considers to be the lost sheep of Israel. The term *Jew* included any person who belonged to one of the original twelve tribes of Israel. The term *Gentile* included everyone else—basically non-Jewish people.

However, one day, Jesus tells His disciples to get in a boat so they can go to the other side of the Sea of Galilee, right into the heart of the Decapolis and where those who worshiped other gods lived. By this, we know that the kingdom of God began to be shared with Gentiles.

**Read Ephesians 2:11–17. Because of Jesus Christ, what is now true of you, a Gentile?**

In Joshua's day, God wrote the Law on tablets of stone to remind the people that it never changes. In Christ, the Word has been written on the tablet of our hearts so that by faith we have the forgiveness of sins and life with Him that never ends.

His covenant of love never fades. Let His praises ring!

## GO QUIET, GO DEEP

Quiet your mind from distractions and pull your Bible close. Bow your head and ask Jesus to make His Word and today's text personal for you.

Take your time writing out 1 John 4:11–12.

What does it mean to you to love others as God loves you?

I pray that the love of Christ leads you to forgive those who have hurt you and love even those who are hard to love.

LESSON 5

# Faith to Stop the Sun and Conquer the Land

*(Joshua 9–12)*

The Israelites continue their mission to conquer the land God promised under Joshua's exceptional leadership. These chapters contain much warfare, some of which may seem hard to understand.

As you read, remember that these chapters have much to teach believers about spiritual warfare. Every day we are at war against an unseen enemy in the heavenly places (Ephesians 6). As you read of each battle and the victories God brings, know that God fights just as valiantly for you today.

DAY 1: The Gibeonite Deception (Joshua 9)

DAY 2: The Sun Stands Still (Joshua 10:1–27)

DAY 3: Conquest of Southern Canaan (Joshua 10:28–43)

DAY 4: Conquest of Northern Canaan (Joshua 11)

DAY 5: Victories of Moses and Joshua (Joshua 12)

**Key Questions:**

- Have you ever intentionally deceived someone or a group of people? If so, how did that impact your spiritual journey and relationship with them?
- What is the most faith-filled and audacious prayer you have ever asked God that He granted?

- How do you believe that your faith would grow if you took the time to actually write down the significant victories God has given to you?

## Day 1

# THE GIBEONITE DECEPTION

*(Joshua 9)*

We turn to a new chapter in the book of Joshua and find the Israelites faithfully on God's mission to conquer the Promised Land. Chapters 9–12 have much to teach believers about spiritual warfare, which can be much more subtle and dreadful than physical combat. Spiritual wars are often won or lost in our minds before we see the results in real time. Deception is a key weapon of the enemy when it comes to spiritual warfare.

**Read Joshua 9:1–15. What stands out to you in these verses?**

The psychological warfare deployed by the Gibeonites stands unique in light of the physical warfare we have studied in previous chapters. The battlefield of this type of warfare resides in the mind rather than the body.

The Israelites' enemies have heard about the miraculous victories that God had given His people at Jericho and Ai. They accurately assess that Joshua and the Israelites pose a great threat. Therefore, they decide to join forces as one coalition to stand against God and His purposes.

Earlier in this study we saw the same principle between Bethel and Ai (page 131). When Joshua ambushed Ai, Bethel's soldiers also came to defend the city of Ai (Joshua 8:17). However, the Gibeonites decide to take a different approach. Rather than form alliances and coalitions with other Canaanite kings, the Gibeonites use cunning and deception on the Israelites.

**According to Joshua 9:3–6, what is the Gibeonite's plan?**

Although the Gibeonites propose to "make a covenant," their deceit (like all deceit) is self-serving.

**Have you ever intentionally deceived someone? If so, what were the circumstances? What was the result?**

Because of our sinful nature, we have all deceived and been deceived. The circumstances and ramifications may vary, but they all show one thing: Self-preservation or saving face is more important to us in those moments than honesty. Our integrity takes a hit in the face of deceit and dishonesty.

What do the following verses teach us about integrity?

**2 Corinthians 8:20–21**

**Proverbs 10:9**

**Proverbs 11:3**

Integrity honors God, and over time He exposes deceit for all to see. Aside from the guilt that comes with deceit, other areas of our life are impacted, including appetite, sleep, stress, and more.

So who are the Gibeonites? They are a conglomeration of people groups who were descendants of Amorites (2 Samuel 21:2). They inhabit various towns of Gibeon located north of Jerusalem. Biblical scholars have placed Gibeon approximately six miles north of Jerusalem, whereas Ai was six miles south. The proximity of the cities makes it likely that the Gibeonites knew about the Israelites' victory at Ai.

Archaeologists have found unique relics that have helped pinpoint the biblical site of Gibeon. Winemaking was a leading industry in Gibeon during Joshua's day. The winemakers used not only wineskins to hold their new wine but also jars as containers. Enterprising vintners inscribed their names, along with the name of the city, on the handles of their wine jars. Approximately thirty jar handles have been discovered to date, confirming that Gibeon (as described in Joshua 9) was located precisely where the Bible states.

The reference to "they" in Joshua 9:4 likely indicates leaders from their various towns. The Gibeonites had hatched their plan of deception and began to set it in motion.

**In Joshua 9:6, what are the Gibeonites' first words to Joshua?**

No preamble. No explanation. No identification. Just a whole lot of nerve. The Israelites are well aware of the serious implications of making a treaty with ungodly people.

**Write out Deuteronomy 7:1–2.**

God's instructions are crystal clear. Treaties with any residents of Canaan are strictly forbidden. Consequently, Joshua and the Israelites question from where these sudden visitors have come.

**In Joshua 9:9, how do the Gibeonites respond?**

They use a key phrase: "because of the name of the LORD your God." The Hebrew word the Gibeonites choose to use for God is the proper name of the one true God, "Yahweh." Similar to Rahab (Joshua 2:9–11), the Gibeonites make an astonishing confession of faith. Scholars have this to say about the Gibeonites' choice:

> Their decision not to fight or flee but to seek a covenant of peace

> with Israel is not based on the relative sizes of the armies or the advantages or disadvantages of their position or defenses. Instead, they undertake their course of action based on *their knowledge of and belief in who Israel's LORD is and his prior acts of judgment and salvation.* [emphasis in original][15]

Similar to Rahab, the Gibeonites make peace with Israel to follow God in order to preserve their lives from destruction. However, they are not the only ones who did so. In 1 Kings 10, the Queen of Sheba sought out Solomon because she had heard of his godly wisdom. She believed in the Lord and became a redeemed believer (Luke 11:31; Matthew 12:42).

**In John 12:20–26, what happens when some Greeks seek out Jesus?**

Scripture is clear about those who call on the name of the Lord. What happens to those who seek the Lord according to the following verses?

**Romans 10:13**

**Acts 2:21**

This beautiful truth is extended to you and me as well. I was baptized after attending church for six months, yet I did not fully understand what it meant to follow God. Thankfully, we grow in grace and understanding over time, through the work of the Holy Spirit in us.

**How have you seen your spiritual growth mature over the years?**

Whether you were baptized as an infant or when you were eighty years old, the power of God faithfully transforms you into the likeness of His Son.

After the Gibeonites confess their faith, they request Joshua to enter into a covenant (or an oath) with them.

**In Joshua 9:14–15, what does Joshua do?**

One eye-opening phrase stands out: "but did not ask counsel from the Lord." Making a covenant or oath is deeply connected to God, who would guarantee the oath and all of its related promises. Surprisingly, Joshua does not consult God.

**How often do you make significant decisions without consulting the Lord? What has been the result?**

When you and I study God's Word and commit portions of it to memory, making decisions based on what the Lord teaches us ensures His continued blessing throughout the process. Joshua fails to consult the Lord and reaps consequences rather than benefits.

**Read Joshua 9:16–27.**

Joshua learns that the Gibeonites are, in fact, their neighbors. Canaanites. The enemy. *Oops.* In those days, a covenant was sworn not only among men but also to God. It could not be broken without serious ramifications, including divine judgment (Leviticus 26:23–25). The Israelites should destroy the Gibeonites, but their newly formed covenant before God prevents it.

The Gibeonites confess their fear of being destroyed and reiterate their confession of faith, putting their fate in Joshua's hands.

**In Joshua 9:27, what does Joshua do with the Gibeonites?**

The Gibeonites present an example of "foreigners" (Gentiles) who are allowed permanent (and in some instances, close) relations with the Israelites. They serve God's people in the home and outside the home, including cut ting wood and drawing water (Joshua 9:23).

Even though the Gibeonites deceived Joshua, they choose to serve the Lord and are spared death. That is God's grace on beautiful display.

When you and I fail to consult the Lord like Joshua or act deceitfully like the Gibeonites, God does not write us off for destruction. Your confession of faith that Jesus is Lord and Savior grants you a place at the Lord's eternal banquet.

Grace upon grace.

## GO QUIET, GO DEEP

Quiet your mind from distractions and pull your Bible close. Bow your head and ask Jesus to make His Word and today's text personal for you.

Take your time writing out Proverbs 12:22.

What does it mean to you to act faithfully?

I pray that your witness about the Lord and His love is one of upright integrity and faithfulness to His teachings.

## DAY 2

# THE SUN STANDS STILL

*(Joshua 10:1–27)*

Situated between the coastal plains near the Mediterranean Sea and the mountains of the central hill country, the Shephelah saw much conflict in antiquity. In this foothill region between Judah's hill country and Philistia's coastal plains, Samson struck down one thousand Philistines with the jawbone of a donkey (Judges 15:15). David felled Goliath with a river stone in one of the Shephelah's valleys (the Valley of Elah) (1 Samuel 17:1–2).

The Shephelah is also the backdrop of one of the boldest prayers recorded in the pages of Scripture. The Valley of Aijalon was a strategic trade route through the northern part of the Shephelah. And it is here where Joshua asks the Lord to make the sun stand still.

As Joshua 10 opens, the known world again prepares to unite against God, His purposes, and His people.

### The Sun Stands Still

**Read Joshua 10:1–5. What stands out to you in these verses?**

After making the covenant with Joshua to serve the Lord, the Gibeonites go back to their city. The five Amorite kings hear about their peace treaty with Israel, so they set their sights on Gibeon for destruction.

**In Joshua 10:2, what do we learn about the city of Gibeon?**

The city of Gibeon is significant. Aside from being a great city full of warriors, 1 Chronicles 21:29 adds that the tabernacle of the Lord, which Moses had made in the wilderness (the tent, not the ark of the covenant), was later located at Gibeon in King David's time. Gibeon is about to learn a crucial lesson that every Christian in his or her early stages of faith needs to understand about walking with God: His enemies come knocking.

Warfare should not come as a surprise when you break away from this world to walk with God. As His beloved child, you are a threat to Satan's misguided and doomed plan of universal domination. Consequently, the enemy will form any harmful coalition necessary to defeat you. He never relinquishes one of his own without a fight. When a person has received the Word of God by faith or even contemplates walking with Jesus, all hell breaks loose. I can attest to that firsthand. Family persecution, threats, temptation, financial difficulty, relationship difficulties, job insecurity—you name it, and the enemy will try it.

Ephesians 6:10–18 lists the pieces of armor that God has given to every believer as protection against the schemes of the enemy.

**From that list, which piece is getting the hardest workout in this season of your life?**

By the grace of God, we do not face our enemies without protection from God. As I write this study, the enemy is lobbing dirty bombs of distraction in my mind. As you encounter spiritual warfare, I encourage you to hide God's Word in your heart. Write out and memorize Ephesians 6:10–18. Each day, recite those pieces of armor to yourself as you dress for the day. It is a powerful way to start any day.

In Joshua 10:5, the five Amorite kings line up against the Gibeonites. We learned in our last session that the Gibeonites were descended from the Amorites (2 Samuel 21:2). That fact adds additional weight to this momentous battle. Due to the Gibeonites' choice to leave the fold and defect, the king of Jerusalem creates a coalition with neighboring pagan kings to declare war against Gibeon.

**Read Joshua 10:6–15. What stands out to you in these verses?**

The Gibeonites are now covenant allies of the Israelites (though by deceptive methods, much like Jacob deceived Isaac to receive God's blessings). They promptly request Joshua's help to ensure the safety and preservation of their city and people. Joshua honors the covenant he had made with Gibeon in the sight of the Lord. Without hesitation, Joshua and his men march through the night from Gilgal to arrive at Gibeon.

Notably, the march from Gilgal to Gibeon was uphill. Literally. The twenty-mile distance between the two cities included an elevation climb of over three thousand feet. It would have taken Joshua and his soldiers between eight and ten hours of arduous, uphill marching.

**What is the hardest thing you have ever had to do to keep a promise?**

**What blessings from God did you see as a result of your faithfulness?**

What do the following verses say about keeping your word?

**1 John 2:5**

**Numbers 30:2**

**Matthew 5:33**

Keeping our word honors God, whom we love and represent. Even in the smallest commitments, honoring the promises we make to others matters.

**According to Joshua 10:8, what does the Lord promise to Joshua?**

In honoring the covenant with Gibeon, Joshua does not make the same mistake as he did when he entered into it. This time, Joshua inquires of the Lord, and God promises victory.

**In Joshua 10:12–13, what famous request does Joshua make of the Lord?**

**Would you have the faith to utter such a daring request? Why or why not?**

As you can imagine, debates over the *physical* possibility of Joshua's request have raged for centuries. Some scholars classify Joshua's request as figurative, poetic, or even metaphorical. Consequently, they dismiss it as literature. Some scholars classify Joshua's request as a pure miracle, meaning that no archaeological or astronomical evidence would be available to back it up. Consequently, they dismiss it as a religious issue, not a fact issue. Others dismiss it as merely the first recorded solar eclipse.

However, you and I believe God's Word is inspired and inerrant. Consequently, we believe by faith that God miraculously prolongs a normal twenty-four-hour day enough to bring Joshua and His people victory at Gibeon.

**What does Genesis 1:1 tell us?**

Our God, who created the heavens and earth out of nothing, also commands them at His pleasure. Martin Luther wrote:

> God's power had been so ordered that the sun retained its course and motion; but when Joshua prayed in his distress and commanded the sun to stand still, the sun stood still at Joshua's word. Ask the astronomers how great a miracle this is! But what is the reason? No other than that God does the will of those who fear Him and subordinates His will to ours, provided we continue to fear Him. . . . In Scripture, there are more evidences of this kind; they prove that God allows Himself to be prevailed upon and subordinates His will to ours. Why, then, are we so remiss in regard to prayer? Why are we without faith to such an extent and so fainthearted, as though our prayer amounted to nothing?[16]

Mic drop. His powerful, faith-filled words beg this question:

**What miracles could happen in your family, our country, and around the world if you dared to ask God for the impossible?**

In the heat of battle to rescue the Gibeonites from destruction, Joshua witnesses a miracle: stones hurled from heaven at the Israelites' enemies with such laser precision that not one Israelite was hit. He witnesses God literally intervening on their behalf in such a monumental way that he prays a monumental prayer: "*Sun, stand still at Gibeon, and moon, in the Valley of Aijalon*" (emphasis added). We can read that and conclude that it is simply an example of the sovereignty of God.

**However, what does Joshua 10:14 say?**

What made this moment powerful is not that God made the sun stand still; rather, it is that God performs this miracle in direct response to the plea of a faith-filled man operating in the will of God. Joshua asks for it and God answers it.

Another mic drop.

### Five Amorite Kings Executed

**Read Joshua 10:16–27.**

The five Amorite kings flee and hide in a cave away from God's sniper stones of wrath. Yet they soon realize that no one can hide from God's perfect justice. Not Jericho. Not Ai. Not them. There is no neutral status with God; we are either a child of God by faith or an enemy of God by the absence of it (John 3:36; 1 Thessalonians 5:9).

God made the sun stand still because Joshua was ALL IN. When all was said and done, the Lord gave Joshua exactly what He promised: victory!

When we are in distress and call upon the Lord, He never hesitates to come to our defense (Psalm 91:15). God has promised us victory through Jesus Christ (1 John 5:4), so we need to be ALL IN—regardless how bloody the battle will be.

**Write out Revelation 20:7–9.**

God wins. And He faithfully leads us to eternal victory. That's how the story ends. That's how our story ends through faith in Jesus Christ.

Final mic drop.

## GO QUIET, GO DEEP

Quiet your mind from distractions and pull your Bible close. Bow your head and ask Jesus to make His Word and today's text personal for you.

Take your time writing out James 4:7.

What does it mean to you to submit yourself to God?

I pray that you are completely confident that as you surrender your life to the Lord, He will fight for you every single day of your life.

## Day 3

# CONQUEST OF SOUTHERN CANAAN

*(Joshua 10:28–43)*

As we move into the rest of Joshua 10, God continues to bring victories to His people as they conquer the Promised Land. Joshua led Israel, but God was the Commander in Chief.

As we look at Israel's southern campaign across the Promised Land, this map will be helpful for you.

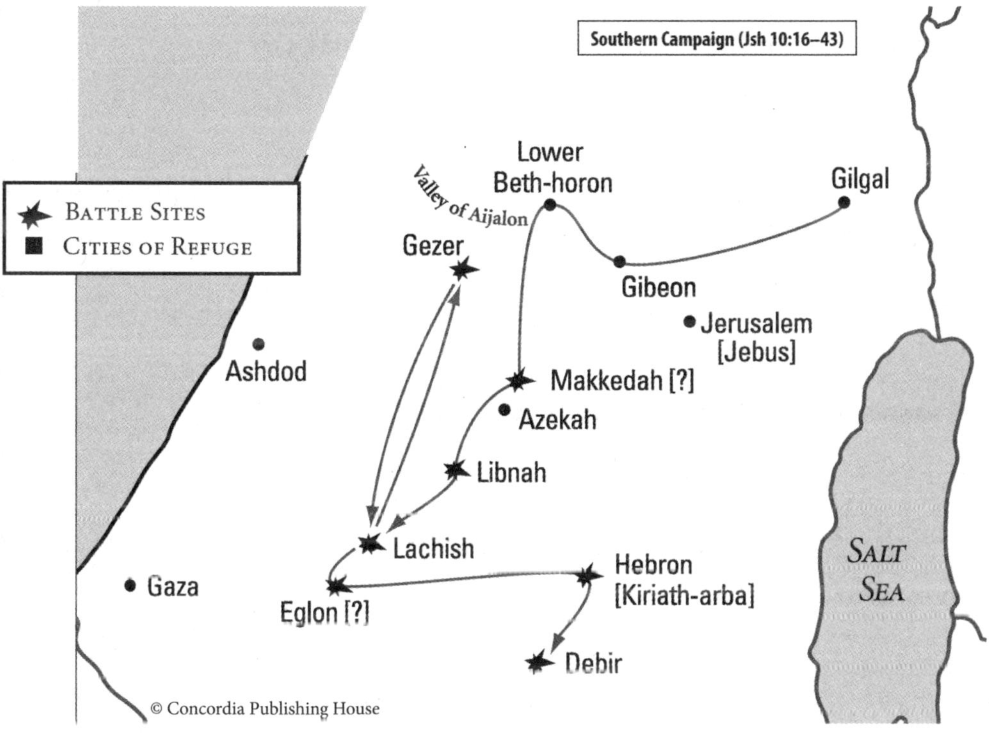




**Read Joshua 10:28–39. What stands out to you in those verses?**

God continues to provide overwhelming victories for Joshua and His people as they clear out the Promised Land to claim their holy inheritance.

After coming to Gibeon's aid, the Israelites continue their southern campaign to Makkedah. Let's look at these southern cities.

**Summarize what happens at Makkedah in Joshua 10:28.**

**Summarize what happens at Libnah in Joshua 10:29–30.**

**Summarize what happens at Lachish in Joshua 10:31–33.**

**Summarize what happens at Eglon in Joshua 10:34–35.**

**Summarize what happens at Hebron in Joshua 10:36–37.**

**Summarize what happens at Debir in Joshua 10:38–39.**

**What similarities do you see in each battle?**

Reading the accounts of so many battles in a row almost numbs the senses—especially when that world is far in time, scope, and relatability from the world in which we live today. However, these few verses represent much warfare spread out over many months.

Even though delineating each battle rather than writing a summary may seem tedious, accurate historical records matter because they tend to reveal patterns and details missed in a cursory summary.

For instance, looking at the map at the beginning of this chapter reveals that Joshua is a brilliant strategic military commander. As they conquer cities by methodically moving south, they cut off any hope of more troops showing up from the enemies' northern pagan allies who had already been conquered and destroyed.

## Weapons of Warfare

Let's take a small detour and talk about the offensive weapons the Israelites would have used. Events in the book of Joshua happened during the Late Bronze Age when warfare was mostly hand-to-hand combat. Joshua 10:28, 8:24, and 24:12 all reference a sword.

This *hereb* used here was a sword-type instrument, the exact shape of which is unspecified. Archaeologists have uncovered both sickle swords and daggers. The sickle-shaped swords were usually the ones used when we read that someone was killed with the "edge of the sword." These sickle swords derived their name from the shape of their long, curved outer edges. Throughout Scripture, the sword is frequently depicted as an agent of God.[17]

The Israelites did not possess (or take possession of) any mechanized weapons during their conquest of the Promised Land. A bow (as in bow and arrow) in Joshua 24:12 is the only other weapon mentioned that was used by God's people.

Also, the topography of the Promised Land's inland did not lend itself to chariots and horses. Rugged and often mountainous terrain would have hindered rather than helped their battle victories.

## Culture's Influence

As discussed earlier in this study, one of the spiritual dangers for the Israelites in the Promised Land was the potential influence of pagan cultures that worshiped idols and false gods. In these battles, we see God effectively destroying pagan altars, destroying idols and their worshipers, and providing a clean slate for His people.

**In your spiritual journey, where have you experienced God "clearing the slate" of idols and things that might distract you from Him?**

**As you think about our modern times, what pagan influence can you see influencing today's culture?**

**How do you believe Christians could be more effective in that regard?**

There is one verse we need to return to for further study.

**Write out Joshua 10:33.**

**Besides the people of Lachish, who does Joshua defeat?**

Horam, the king of Gezer, rules the most powerful city in the area. God's people defeat the king and Gezer's warriors, but the city of Gezer itself is not listed among those conquered. But the citizens of Gezer appear later in the story.

**What does Joshua 16:10 reveal?**

Even though the ruler, warriors, and people of Gezer were defeated, God preserves the city to serve as a ready-made home to some of God's people. This explains why that city is not devoted to complete destruction at that time.

**According to 1 Kings 9:16, what is the eventual fate of Gezer?**

Seven cities are conquered in the Israelites' southern campaign. Again, we see the number *7* (which symbolically represents completion) as Joshua claims victory for the Lord.

**Read Joshua 10:40–43. What stands out to you in those verses?**

Goshen, mentioned in 10:41, is not the Goshen in Egypt from the days of Joseph or of Moses. Rather, the Goshen referred to here was an area in the eastern Negev.

Joshua has led God's people to a resounding victory over southern Canaan. Scholars estimate that it took between twelve and fourteen months to complete. So it is time to rest and return to their camp at Gilgal, where they camped after first crossing the Jordan.

You and I have the incredible blessing of being suited up in God's armor to face life's battles, knowing that Jesus brings complete victory. It took Jesus living a perfect life for thirty-three years to prepare that victory on our behalf. Easter morning confirmed instant victory for all who believe that Jesus conquered death.

In His great love for us, while we battle the forces of evil in the heavenly places in this life (see Ephesians 6:12), God has faithfully equipped us for every challenge to secure ultimate victory on our behalf.

There is no greater victory!

## GO QUIET, GO DEEP

Quiet your mind from distractions and pull your Bible close. Bow your head and ask Jesus to make His Word and today's text personal for you.

Take your time writing out 1 John 5:4.

What does it mean to you that God has already given you eternal victory through faith in Jesus Christ?

I pray that the victory God has given you in Christ is the cornerstone of how you live, serve, and tell others about Jesus.

DAY 4

# CONQUEST OF NORTHERN CANAAN

*(Joshua 11)*

Our last session navigated through Joshua's conquest of seven cities in southern Canaan. God brought them complete victory and they returned to their camp at Gilgal to rest and recuperate before the northern campaign began.

Throughout Joshua 11, the Israelites continue their systematic victories through Canaan, where Joshua comes face to face with his past. You will find this map helpful as we dive in.

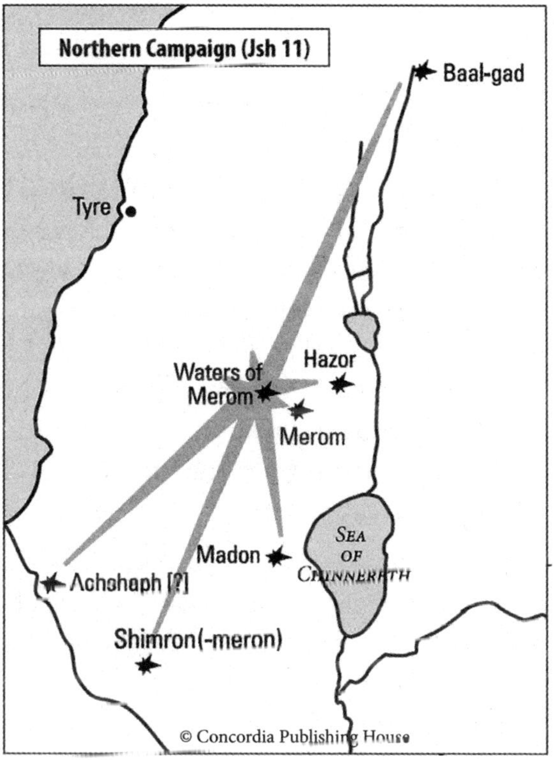


**Read Joshua 11:1–5.**

The author provides clear boundaries of northern Canaan along with a glimpse into the mindset of its inhabitants before Joshua and his men arrive. Again, we see the kings joining forces as they garner troops to face the Lord's army.

However, the northern coalition of cities would comprise the most difficult and formidable battles to date for God's people.

**In Joshua 11:4, how are the northern forces described?**

Many of the cities' armies have horses and chariots, whereas Joshua's men are foot soldiers. The northern cities also contain very diverse peoples who reflect an international culture with commercial influence (which Scripture reflects later in the northern kingdom of Israel).

In human terms, these battles will not be easy. In God's terms, the victory is already won.

**What location is mentioned at the end of Joshua 11:5?**

The waters of Merom (known today as Hula Lake) sit in the lush and beautiful Hula Valley in the Upper Galilee region. It is one of the world's oldest recorded lakes (some even say the oldest). Today, the Hula Valley is one of the world's premier birdwatching sites. I visited the Hula Valley for the first time in December 2022 with a group I had taken to the Holy Land for a biblical tour. Each autumn, approximately five hundred million migrating birds fly through Israel on their way to Africa from Europe, then make the return trip in the spring. That migration is larger than any country in the world outside of Panama.

As the sun was setting over Hula Lake, our group climbed aboard a large safari-type vehicle. We drove slowly through the bird fields as thousands of birds were coming in to roost for the night around Hula Lake. After a busy day of touring Magdala and Capernaum, it was a peaceful respite for us to experience such beauty amid God's creation.

When Joshua and the Israelites arrive to face the northern coalition, the scene at Hula Lake (the waters of Merom) is quite different.

**Read Joshua 11:6–15. What are the first words God says in Joshua in 11:6?**

The Israelites are about to face the most well-armed and experienced armies of all their battles to date. Nevertheless, God reminds Joshua not to be afraid of them. No matter how well the enemy is outfitted, God still wins.

**What situations in your life tend to cause you the most fear?**

**How do you prepare for those situations?**

Arming yourself with the Word of the Lord is the best way to alleviate fear and remind yourself of who is truly in charge.

Write out the following verses and keep them handy for those fear-inducing situations:

**Psalm 23:4**

**Isaiah 41:13**

**Luke 12:7**

God reminds us (and Joshua) not to be afraid because He will faithfully supply everything He has promised for those who believe.

**As a result of God's promise in Joshua 11:6, what does Joshua do in 11:7?**

Joshua wastes no time. The Lord promised victory, so Joshua immediately charges Israel's enemies to surprise them at the waters of Merom.

Before writing this study, I had never bothered to look up what it meant to "hamstring" a horse. Growing up with horses gave me a special love for that noble, beautiful animal. I assumed that to hamstring a horse meant to kill it indiscriminately. The mere thought of that turned my stomach sour. Not so! It means to cut certain tendons on a horse's back legs so they are unable to carry heavy loads. That means those horses could still be used for farming. However, they could no longer carry soldiers into battle.

**What city is mentioned in Joshua 11:10?**

Significantly, Hazor is the largest city in Canaan, with a population of approximately twenty thousand people. That is one of the reasons Hazor is referred to as the "head of all those kingdoms." Hazor has an upper city (acropolis) that spans approximately twenty-six acres and a lower city that spans approximately one hundred and twenty-six acres. It is heavily fortified with stone and mud brick walls as wide as twenty-four feet.

Archaeologists are certain they have pinpointed the exact location of Hazor because a tourist in 1962 discovered a clay tablet at the site with the name of the city on it.[18]

**In Joshua 11:11, what does Joshua do to Hazor?**

Like many of the cities the Israelites had already conquered, God had devoted Hazor to destruction. Therefore, Joshua burns the city after the Israelites' conquered it.

Archaeologists have discovered several places at the Hazor site containing evidence of destruction by fire. The three temples that have been excavated were violently destroyed. This confirms Exodus 34:13, "You shall tear down their altars and break their pillars and cut down their Asherim."

**Read Joshua 11:16–23. What stands out to you in those verses?**

Chapter 11 ends by stating that Joshua had fulfilled all the Lord commanded through Moses. Then the land had rest from war. Finally!

We may tend to think that the story is over, but the Israelites' mission is incomplete. They entered the land and conquered it but have not yet parceled it out and settled in it.

**What are three main things you learned over the past several sessions regarding warfare and God's promises?**

**1.**

**2.**

**3.**

## GO QUIET, GO DEEP

Quiet your mind from distractions and pull your Bible close. Bow your head and ask Jesus to make His Word and today's text personal for you.

Take your time writing out Proverbs 29:25.

What does it mean to you to trust in the Lord even when you are afraid?

I pray that, regardless of your circumstances, the Lord gives you His strength to trust Him without hesitation.

## Day 5

# VICTORIES OF MOSES AND JOSHUA

*(Joshua 12)*

At long last, the Promised Land is at rest from war. Joshua and the Israelites saw the mighty works of God on their behalf. God systematically gave them staggering victories over their enemies. Now they will enjoy a time of much-deserved rest.

All of the battles we have studied over the last several sessions have contained much violence. Seeing the wrath of God on full display may have been as disturbing for you as it was for me. But I offer this thought for you to consider: Because of Jesus Christ, you and I will never see the wrath of God in our own lives.

Now that the battles are over and the parceling out of land is about to begin, there is a burning question that we need to address. It is the proverbial elephant sitting smack dab in the middle of this whole conquering narrative.

### Why the Canaanites?

**Why do you believe God declared war on the Canaanites in the first place?**

The answer starts back in Genesis 12 when God called Abram.

**Write out Genesis 12:1–2.**

Then in Genesis 15, God made a covenant with Abram.

**Write out Genesis 15:7.**

Later in Genesis, God told Abram that after the Israelites have suffered (Egypt), God would bring them back to the land in the fourth generation.

**Write out Genesis 15:16.**

The Canaanites' iniquity or sin had become increasingly morally corrupt over the centuries—particularly when it came to sexual practices (Leviticus 18). Also, they practiced child sacrifice (Deuteronomy 12). When their iniquity reached its zenith, God made good on His promise and prepared Joshua to lead the charge.

God does not want such morally repulsive practices to influence His people, so He systematically removes the Canaanites from the land that He had promised to His people through Abraham. After all, the "why" of warfare is to impose a new way of life.

The Israelites are first told to drive out the Canaanites, then to completely destroy them so "there was none left that breathed." We may find such a command disturbing and extreme. But consider this. God follows those commands in Deuteronomy 7 with warnings to His people not to intermarry or enter into business deals with the Canaanites. How could they marry or make business deals with a people group if they have been completely destroyed?

In Joshua 10:36–39, the Israelites destroyed Hebron and Debir and "left none remaining." However, in Joshua 15:13–15, those cities are still populated by Canaanites. Even though cities and significant strongholds were destroyed, there were likely nomadic people or very small townships that remained, some of which may have relocated to the destroyed cities.

Taking all of this into account, God did not order genocide. After all, the Gibeonites (who were Canaanites) turned to God and were not destroyed. The same was true about Rahab and her family. God remained then and remains today open to bring salvation to all those who will turn to Him.

God had given the Canaanites centuries to repent. They had steadfastly refused. Time is up.

**What is God's purpose in declaring war on the Canaanites according to Deuteronomy 7:6–9?**

God's love for His people reigned supreme then and still does today. He is our faithful Promise Keeper. Although God may never call you to serve in a physical battle, He continually fights on your behalf in spiritual battles that you cannot physically see. He removes roadblocks and influences situations so that His perfect will is brought about in your life—just as He did with Joshua and the Israelites.

### The List of Defeated Kings

Joshua 12 is a significant transition for God's people as they move from conquering the land to settling in the land. But before parceling out their inherited land, God reminds His people of the victories won and peoples conquered.

**Read Joshua 12:1–6.**

These verses delineate the defeated kings and conquered lands under the leadership of Moses on the east side of the Jordan River.

**Why do you believe this would be important for God to point out?**

It is always helpful to remember our history. Where we came from and our past experiences form a significant part of who God has formed us to be today.

**Take a moment to reflect on your history. What do you believe has been the most significant milestone that has shaped who you are today?**

**How do you see God's fingerprints over your life in that milestone?**

The most significant, life-changing milestone in my life was becoming a Christian. I remember my Baptism. I even remember what I chose to wear for that momentous occasion. (Is that a woman thing?) More important, I vividly remembered what it was like to NOT have Jesus in my life. I remember the hopelessness and darkness lodged in my soul. Thanks to the grace of God and His gift of faith, His hope and light are now my daily mainstays.

Receiving the gift of faith as an adult has given me a heart for those who do not know Jesus. I understand their struggles, strivings, and questions of if there is more to life. I truly believe that is why God has given me such a passion for studying His Word. Him equipping me to share His hope and light is the greatest joy of my entire life.

Since context is important, God takes time to remind His people in Joshua 12 where they came from under the leadership of Moses.

From Joshua 12:1–5, which kings were defeated and what land was acquired under Moses on the east side of the Jordan River?

| Kings Defeated by Moses | Land Gained by Moses |
|---|---|
| | |
| | |
| | |
| | |
| | |
| | |
| | |

This list summarizes the kings that Israel defeated. Only two kings ruled on the east side of the Jordan. Each of those two kings ruled a vast area that contained many cities.

**In Joshua 12:6, who receives the land conquered on the east side of the Jordan?**

Those two and one-half tribes requested that Moses grant that land to them because it was ideal for their herds and flocks. With that list as a reminder, God now moves into their more recent military campaigns.

**From Joshua 12:7–24, which kings are defeated under Joshua on the west side of the Jordan River?**

| Kings Defeated by Joshua | Land Gained by Joshua |
|---|---|
| | Vast majority of the Promised Land |
| | |
| | |
| | |
| | |
| | |
| | |

Moses conquered two kings while Joshua conquered thirty-one. It would be easy to say that Joshua won. But these battles were never about a contest of who could take out the most kings or conquer the most square miles. These battles were about God keeping His promise to His people. He equipped the right leaders with the right skills at the right times to achieve it. It is truly astonishing how God transformed a former slave into one of Israel's greatest leaders.

**What skills has God equipped you with over time to accomplish His purposes?**

None of these battle stories are intended to endorse violence in the name of God. These accounts demonstrate how God brought justice to human evil at a particular moment in history. They show how God delivered His people from being annihilated by the Canaanites to bring them into the land He had promised them centuries earlier.

Every believer in every generation benefits from taking time to pause and remember where the Lord has faithfully brought them in their faith journey.

**What has God changed in your faith journey today that was not present a year ago?**

**What are the blessings and challenges of that change?**

The God who was faithful to Moses is the same God who was faithful to Joshua. The God who was faithful to Elijah is the same God who was faithful to Elisha. The God who was faithful to David is the same God who was faithful to Solomon. The God who was faithful to Paul is the same God who was faithful to Timothy. And the God who was faithful to all of them is the same God who is faithful to us. Our journey is safe in His holy hands.

## GO QUIET, GO DEEP

Quiet your mind from distractions and pull your Bible close. Bow your head and ask Jesus to make His Word and today's text personal for you.

Take your time writing out Hebrews 10:23.

What does it mean to you to remember God's faithfulness in your life?

As God continues His faithful work in your life, I pray that your thankfulness is evident to Him and all those around you.

LESSON 6

# VICTORY AND PARCELING OUT THE PROMISED LAND

*(Joshua 13–19)*

The major battles are done and the land of Israel is theirs. However, God tells Joshua there is still more land to possess. God lays out what parts of the Promised Land are yet to be conquered starting geographically in the south and working north. Yet, as He promised, the land of Israel belongs to them, and God begins to delineate how it should be divided among the tribes.

Even though God has brought them into the land He promised, Hebrews 4:1–13 reveals that they do not enter His rest. It is not a land of rest; it is a land to settle and fight for. Today, believers enter God's promised rest in Christ alone. We are not saved by doing good works to make us right with God, but we rest in the finished work of Christ.

The work Joshua began will be finished by others. That is a sobering reality for every leader. The work that we begin by faith will be completed by others after we are home in eternity. Even though God buries His workmen, His work goes on. We run the race and keep the faith, entrusting the future to God alone.

DAY 1: Land Inheritance in the Promised Land (Joshua 13:1–14:5)

DAY 2: Caleb's Inheritance (Joshua 14:6–15)

DAY 3: Land Allotment for Judah (Joshua 15)

DAY 4: Land Allotment for Ephraim and Manasseh (Joshua 16–17)

DAY 5: Allotment of the Remaining Land (Joshua 18–19)

## Key Questions:

- What inheritance has God given to you through faith?
- Why was Caleb allotted a special inheritance apart from the twelve tribes?
- As you read through the land allotments, what strikes you about God's faithfulness?

## DAY 1

# LAND INHERITANCE IN THE PROMISED LAND

*(Joshua 13:1–14:5)*

At the age of 40, Agatha Christie married prominent British archaeologist Max Mallowan in 1930. Afterward, she spent several months each year traveling with her husband to archaeological digs in the Middle East. Leveraging her first-hand acquired knowledge of the Middle East, including Ur, Syria, and Egypt, she became one of the most well-known, beloved, and best-selling detective novelists of all time. And she was no spring chicken! Sometimes it is hard to age gracefully when the world around us sees only our wrinkles.

Joshua 13 opens by saying that Joshua is now "old and advanced in years." That would not be a politically correct label today.

However, the writer is focused on Joshua's faithful service, not a sagging jawline. Joshua has fought long and hard in the Lord's service, and now the time for parceling out the land is upon them. God reminds Joshua of the land that still needs to be conquered and the stipulation that the eastern tribes would fight to help the rest of God's people conquer the land.

**Read Joshua 13:1–7. Which land still needed to be conquered?**

Despite all the kings and lands God has led them to conquer up to this point, God tells His people that much work remains to be done to completely fulfill His promises.

The same could be said of His people today. God has conquered sin and death through Jesus Christ, yet much remains for us to do in His name according to His promises.

According to the following verses, what work has God called us to do?

**1 Peter 2:21**

**Matthew 6:24**

Every work and vocation to which God calls us is filtered through His work in our own lives. He provides the strength and grace to do every single task. Just remember these three important facts: (1) Jesus is our boss, (2) God works through our work, and (3) we can trust God with our work.

**What does Colossians 3:23 tell us?**

When you work for the Lord and in the strength of His might, age is just a number. Whether you are eight years old or eighty, God's work in and through you is not finished.

### Inheritance East of the Jordan

**Read Joshua 13:8–33.**

According to these verses, what land was given by Moses to the two and one-half tribes that remained on the east side of the Jordan?

| TRIBE | LAND |
| --- | --- |
| Reuben: | |
| Gad: | |
| Half Tribe of Manasseh: | |

These two and one-half tribes that had already settled on the east of the Jordan River received their inheritances first according to the Lord's promises. Now that the land rests from war, the fighting men of the eastern tribes will finally have a chance to return home to stay with their families. At long last they can begin to build their new lives with gratitude for the Lord's faithfulness.

**What are you grateful for in this season of life?**

**How can you see the Lord's hand of blessing upon it?**

Viewing the Lord's blessings through the lens of gratitude makes all the difference.

### INHERITANCE WEST OF THE JORDAN

**Read Joshua 14:1–5. In Joshua 14:4, why do the Levites receive no portion?**

**Take a moment to write out Joshua 13:33.**

The Levites do not have any physical land inheritance because the Lord Himself was their inheritance. God does not give the Levites the land but rather the Lord of the land. Can you imagine a greater inheritance? Powerful! Even though God is gracious to provide us with relationships and material goods, the Lord Himself is our inheritance through faith.

Write out the following verses which confirm that beautiful truth:

**Ephesians 1:11–14**

**Romans 8:17**

**Ezekiel 44:28**

Our inheritance in Christ is nothing we had to pay for, work toward, or even ask for. It is God's gracious gift to us and to all who believe by faith that He is Lord.

Thank You, Jesus.

## GO QUIET, GO DEEP

Quiet your mind from distractions and pull your Bible close. Bow your head and ask Jesus to make His Word and today's text personal for you.

Take your time writing out 1 Peter 1:3–5.

What does it mean to you that your most treasured inheritance is the Lord Himself?

I pray that God's mercy and grace continue to saturate your life as one of God's precious heirs.

## DAY 2

# CALEB'S INHERITANCE

*(Joshua 14:6–15)*

Understanding the meaning of an inheritance was not something I grasped as a child. I grew up in an average, middle-class family with no expectation of receiving an overly extravagant inheritance from my parents.

Then, working in a law firm for thirty years did not leave me with a positive impression of inheritances or those who unethically wrangle to receive them. When it comes to who gets what and when in probate court, the battles can get bloody. Sometimes, the attorneys' fees used up all of an estate's money fighting over which family member received which set of tea cups.

I must confess that approaching a deep-dive study of this section of the book of Joshua caused some trepidation. People can lose all sense of reality when it comes to real estate inheritances. However, it was refreshing to see the people of God act in the grace of God as they received the gifts of God in the form of land inheritances.

God's people east of the Jordan have received their requested inheritance from the Lord. Their lush pastures are perfect for their herds and crops. Today's portion of Scripture begins the task of parceling out the Promised Land to the remaining tribes settling on the west side of the Jordan.

But before that process begins, one person deserves special attention: Caleb. Caleb was the only man besides Joshua who the Lord had preserved through the Israelites' desert wanderings.

Only Joshua and Caleb had trusted the Lord and urged Moses and God's people to enter the land. Caleb was only one of two men who had seen the totality of what God had done for His people.

**In Numbers 13:30, what did Caleb tell Moses, Aaron, and God's people?**

Caleb urged the people to follow God's promise into the land, but the people (other than he and Joshua) cowered and did not enter Canaan. There are two important insights we can discern from this verse. First, Caleb's God-given leadership skills are already evident in this verse. He was bold enough to ask the people to quiet down so they could hear his report. The fact that the people obeyed his request demonstrates that Caleb possessed a measure of authority. Perhaps the people had learned from experience that when Caleb spoke, his words were worth hearing.

**Has God blessed you with someone in your life whose wise words are worth hearing? If so, who and why?**

God has blessed me with a handful of dear, godly friends who fall into that category. They are the ones whom I call when I need spiritual wisdom on any given topic. They are calm, patient people who do not leap to conclusions without facts, do not anger quickly, and do not provide feedback before giving the issue proper thought.

The world is full of people who are full of opinions and willing to share them, whether we want to hear them or not. I truly cherish those "safe place" friends with whom I can talk through spiritual issues, knowing that their words are worth hearing.

Second, Caleb's words in Numbers 13:30 demonstrate his complete faith in God's promises. God said they could enter and conquer the Promised Land and, like Joshua, Caleb was ALL IN. This demonstrates a maturity of faith essential in any leader.

**In Numbers 14:30, what did God decree regarding Caleb and Joshua?**

**What did God specifically say about Caleb in Numbers 14:24?**

Thirty-eight years after Caleb and Joshua scoped out the Promised Land, God's promise to bring His people into it has come to fruition. They fought for seven years to conquer the land in the Lord's strength. God is now ready to give Caleb an inheritance in the Promised Land for his faithful service.

At eighty-five years old, Caleb approaches Joshua at Gilgal.

**Read Joshua 14:6–12. What stands out to you in these verses?**

Caleb recalls the course of events that brought them to the current moment in time and makes an important statement of faith: "I wholly followed the Lord my God." Caleb does not refer to God as the God of the people or even Joshua's God. Caleb knows the Lord as *"my God."*

**In your walk with the Lord, can you confidently say that God is *your* God? Why or why not?**

Our limited human minds can never truly grasp the immensity of God's glory. We cannot fully understand the fullness of His character. Yet even though God is incomprehensibly magnificent, He is also personal and relational. Matthew 1:23 reminds us that He is Immanuel, God with us. In 2 Corinthians 3, the apostle Paul makes clear that Jesus' sacrifice and the Spirit's indwelling make such a personal relationship with God possible. A personal relationship with God through Christ is the greatest blessing of all time for all people.

As much as Caleb could grasp, he understands that God is personally "my God." And he is unafraid to say it out loud.

**In Joshua 14:12, what does Caleb propose?**

After years of fighting, Caleb is willing to take on yet another enemy in order to receive his preferred inheritance location. These inhabitants are not just any enemy but the Anakim. The Anakim are a race of giants who are descendants of the Nephilim (the giants whom Caleb and Joshua encountered decades earlier as spies).

At eighty-five years old and with the strength of a much younger man, Caleb is still willing to go the extra mile for the Lord.

**At this stage in your life, how willing are you to go the extra mile in serving the Lord? What would that look like?**

Most days, my answer is a resounding yes. Then there are those exhausting days you barely make it through when my yes is not as enthusiastic. Can you relate?

**Read Joshua 14:13–15.**

Caleb finally receives his inheritance in Hebron because he wholly followed the Lord. Interestingly, the word *Hebron* means friend or comrade. Abraham was known as a "friend of God" (James 2:23). Caleb was indeed a friend of God. Abraham, Isaac, Jacob, and their wives are buried at Hebron in the cave of Machpelah. Consequently, Hebron is one of the most holy sites for Jews today.

**What is the final sentence of Joshua 14:15?**

Similar to Joshua 11:23, we are reminded that after seven long, hard-fought years, the land finally rests from war. What God had promised has come to pass. Caleb is ready to rest from war and enjoy his allotted inheritance from the Lord.

Praise God, from whom all blessings flow (*LSB* 805).

## GO QUIET, GO DEEP

Quiet your mind from distractions and pull your Bible close. Bow your head and ask Jesus to make His Word and today's text personal for you.

Take your time writing out Proverbs 27:9.

What does it mean to you to have "safe place" friends in your life who offer godly wisdom as you walk through life together?

I pray that God nurtures in you the gift of being a "safe place" friend to others as well.

## DAY 3

# LAND ALLOTMENT FOR JUDAH

*(Joshua 15)*

The immeasurable blessing of owning your own piece of land cannot be fully comprehended. The landscape and gardens around my little Texas cottage have changed significantly from when I first moved in six years ago. I have added many flower beds, eight raised vegetable beds, blackberry and blueberry bushes, fruit trees, an arbor of wisteria, a bird bath, small piles of wood here and there along the perimeter fence to encourage wildlife to visit, and plenty of pollinator plants to benefit them all.

Morning strolls in the gardens are my favorite. The dew-covered freshness and gentle sunlight invite me to slow my pace to notice every flower petal and each emerging baby vegetable as I listen to the songbirds. The feral cats always greet me to receive their breakfast before disappearing again.

Since the weather turns blazing hot in the summer, I try to knock out any significant gardening tasks before noon. There is always something to do and a new blessing to discover in this piece of land the Lord has entrusted to me. There is just something about home.

As we continue our study through the book of Joshua, we turn our attention to the tribal allotments on the west side of the Jordan. Our previous session showed how Caleb, Joshua's faithful leader, was the first to receive his inheritance. Now let's dive in to see home for the western tribes.

**Read Joshua 15:1–12.**

These verses set the boundaries that will mark Judah's land inheritance. There is an important word that we need to understand before moving any further.

**Write out Joshua 15:1.**

The word *allotment* is often translated as *lot.* By using this particular word, the author reveals that the land is being parceled out through the casting of lots. This process was also used by the guards at Jesus' crucifixion to determine who received His garment. Casting lots to determine various outcomes was a common practice in biblical times.

**Write out Joshua 18:10.**

Here we see confirmation of the use of casting lots to determine the tribal inheritance. We will dive deeper into the meaning of casting lots when we get to Joshua 18.

Also in this land allotment process that we will study over the next few sessions, we often see the words *inheritance* and *allotment* used interchangeably.

**Write out Joshua 13:6.**

This particular verse uses both *allot* and *inheritance.* The word *inheritance* carries a greater meaning than merely a gift of generosity. It contains a legal connotation that means the recipient is receiving his rightfully held portion. God promised each tribe a rightful portion of the Promised Land as an inheritance. Conversely, casting lots to determine a tribe's allotment was a process that occurred *within* their inherited portion of the Promised Land.

With those definitions tucked into the back of our minds, let's continue where we left off in Joshua 15.

**Read Joshua 15:13–19. What stands out to you in these verses?**

Here, we see Caleb's inheritance mentioned for a second time. We learn for the first time that Caleb's allotment is within the boundaries of Judah's allotment. Caleb has driven out the Anakim (the people of Anak) just as he promised Joshua. From there, Caleb sets his sights on Debir in the Negeb.

**Write out Joshua 15:16.**

Caleb does not want Debir for himself but as a blessing for his daughter Achsah and his soon-to-be son-in-law, whose identity will be determined by who conquers the city.

We see in Joshua 15:17 that the man who conquers Debir is identified as "Othniel the son of Kenaz, the brother of Caleb." Does that mean Achsah married a male relative?

> It is not clear from the Hebrew here . . . . whether Othniel is Caleb's nephew or his younger brother. However, the genealogy of [1 Chronicles] 4:13–15 has parallel accounts of the sons of Kenaz and of the sons of Caleb, which suggests that Kenaz and Caleb were brothers. So if "brother of Caleb" here in [Joshua] 15:17 goes with Kenaz, then Othniel is Caleb's nephew (the son of his brother Kenaz). Achsah, daughter of Caleb, thus marries her cousin.[19]

It was not uncommon in biblical times for families to intermarry to preserve an inheritance or bloodline. Leviticus 18:6–18 provides the law on who a man is not allowed to marry, and a cousin is not on the list. In fact, Jacob married Rachel and Leah, who were his cousins (Genesis 28). Of course, that was before the law against marrying two sisters was given!

Caleb's daughter requests the "springs of water" in a field of the land of Negeb where Debir is located. This provides an insight into the beautiful topography of that location. Debir possesses ample pasturelands and is later designated as one of the Levitical tribe allotments.

**Read Joshua 15:20–63.**

Here we see an impressive list of the cities contained within Judah's inheritance. Below is a handy reference table to understand the scope of the land given to the tribe of Judah:

| Scripture | Land Location |
|---|---|
| Joshua 15:21–32 | The cities of Judah in the Negev |
| Joshua 15:33–47 | The cities of Judah in the Shephelah |
| Joshua 15:48–60 | The cities of Judah in the hill country |
| Joshua 15:61–62 | The cities in Judah's wilderness |

**According to Genesis 49:8–12, how is the tribe of Judah described?**

The tribe of Judah would be a warrior tribe (like a lion) and a kingly tribe (the scepter not departing from it, pointing to the Messiah). To subdue and maintain control of that vast amount of land and cities, the tribe that inherits them would certainly need to be warriors. Looking at the map at the beginning of this study, Judah inherits the largest allotment by far since it is the largest tribe among the twelve.

**If you had to map out the blessings—whether tangible or intangible—that the Lord has allotted to you, what would that map contain?**

As we wrap up chapter 15, Joshua 15:63 notes a very important detail: Judah controls all of the land *except* Jerusalem. The capture and control of Jerusalem would not happen until the time of King David.

It must have been extraordinary to each tribe that the land for which they had fought for so long was now theirs. Through the promises and grace of God, they would now have land in which God's immeasurable blessings of home, trade, and family could be fully enjoyed.

## GO QUIET, GO DEEP

Quiet your mind from distractions and pull your Bible close. Bow your head and ask Jesus to make His Word and today's text personal for you.

Take your time writing out Psalm 127:1a.

What does it mean to you to let the Lord build your house?

I pray that the place you call home is a place where His name and fame are cherished and lifted high.

## Day 4

# LAND ALLOTMENT FOR EPHRAIM AND MANASSEH

*(Joshua 16–17)*

The tribes of Ephraim and Manasseh are unique among the tribes of Israel. The other eleven tribes are named after one of Jacob's twelve sons. The twelfth tribe is comprised of these two half-tribes that went to the grandsons of Jacob.

Genesis 37–50 provides an extraordinary account of the life of Joseph, the father of Ephraim and Manasseh. Joseph went from being the favorite son of his father Jacob to being sold into slavery by his older brothers to then being elevated as second in command over all of Egypt, where he used his skills to save God's people from perishing in a devastating famine. Through it all, Joseph remained faithful to God. God used Joseph to settle His people in a land of plenty.

Ephraim and Manasseh were the sons of Joseph. As a double blessing for Joseph's faithfulness, rather than grant Joseph his own tribe like his eleven brothers, God gave each of Joseph's sons a half-tribe that together made up one of the twelve tribes.

> Out of all the Old Testament cast of characters, Joseph offers us a remarkable picture of Jesus. In my opinion, he more closely models Christ than any other. In countless ways, the life of Joseph parallels the future life of Jesus. Specifically, Joseph
>
> - was a shepherd deeply loved by his father;
> - was hated and rejected by his brothers; . . .
> - was sold for pieces of silver and turned over to Gentiles;
> - endured severe temptation but did not sin;
> - was accused falsely but spoke no defense; . . .
> - married a Gentile bride; [and] . . .

- became the only source of bread for the world.[20]

After his brothers effectively stole his life, it would have been easy for Joseph to become bitter and angry. Yet in all circumstances, Joseph trusted God, and in doing so, God promised to bless his two sons, Ephraim and Manasseh.

**What does Genesis 49:22–26 reveal about Joseph?**

The blessing that Jacob pronounced over his son Joseph is the longest one—even longer than the blessing over Judah. Because of Joseph's deep, abiding faith to walk in God's ways, God gave to him more abundantly than his brothers through material blessings, including agriculture and a large family.

Part of God's blessings now includes land allotments in the Promised Land for both of Joseph's sons.

**Read Joshua 16:1–4. How is the inheritance of Joseph's sons described in Joshua 16:4?**

God had never forgotten Joseph's faithfulness. Even though the tribes were named Ephraim and Manasseh, they were "*the people of Joseph*" (emphasis added).

**Have you ever been referred to as the relative of someone in your family? If so, who and why?**

I first experienced this when my older sister and I spent summers with one of our grandmothers in Arkansas. Anytime we would walk into town to visit a shop or have an ice cream cone, people would refer to us as "Gertrude's granddaughters from Texas." My grandmother was a respected citizen in her small town, so it felt good to be accepted by her friends and acquaintances.

In Joshua 16:2, Luz is mentioned as part of the allotment for "the people of Joseph." Even though the town of Luz was its original name, it was later changed to Bethel (Genesis 28:19). Joseph's father Jacob, grandfather to Ephraim and Manasseh, had slept at Bethel where God appeared to him in the dream of angels ascending and descending a ladder between heaven and earth. What a cool family connection!

## Tribal Allotments for Ephraim

**Read Joshua 16:5–10.**

Ephraim's allotment contains mostly hill country in the heart of the Promised Land. Having visited there, I can say it is truly a beautiful landscape. I can only imagine the wonder and delight of Ephraim's tribe as they saw their inherited portion for the first time.

**What does Joshua 16:10 tell us?**

Similar to Judah failing to drive out the Canaanites from Jerusalem, the tribe of Ephraim fails to drive out the Canaanites from Gezer. However, their military prowess shines through as they eventually possess the city and subdue the Canaanites into forced labor.

## Tribal Allotments for Manasseh

**Read Joshua 17:1–18.**

The borders of Manasseh cover a huge area of land, stretching to the Jordan River on the east. Consequently, this description does not include the land already allotted to the half-tribe of Manasseh located east of the Jordan.

Only the tribe of Judah received a larger land inheritance.

These verses reveal a unique issue that Manasseh must contend with: Parts of their land inheritance still remained in Canaanite hands and were not conquered by the Israelites (Joshua 17:12). Joshua 17:13 also reveals that part of the land that had been conquered by the Israelites was still inhabited by Canaanites who had become slave laborers (an arrangement similar to the Gibeonites' mentioned earlier in our study). But there is more.

That section of Scripture also tells us that Manasseh could not take possession of some cities because "the Canaanites persisted in dwelling in that land" (17:12). This points to a spiritual weakness in the tribe of Manasseh.

**What insight into your spiritual walk can you derive from Manasseh's situation?**

As long as you and I are here on earth, we have enemies in our midst. I am not referring to a difficult coworker or cantankerous neighbor.

**What does 1 Peter 5:8 tell us?**

Only our Lord and Savior Jesus Christ can completely defeat the enemies of heaven and earth. Until that day, we keep our eyes plastered on Him in faith and trust that the places He plants our feet are exactly where they are supposed to be.

## GO QUIET, GO DEEP

Quiet your mind from distractions and pull your Bible close. Bow your head and ask Jesus to make His Word and today's text personal for you.

Take your time writing out Colossians 2:15.

What does it mean to you that Jesus has already triumphed over your enemies?

I pray that Jesus' triumph provides you the daily courage to walk in His strength regardless of your enemies.

## DAY 5

# ALLOTMENT OF THE REMAINING LAND

*(Joshua 18–19)*

When my three sisters and I were kids, our parents were very careful to not show favoritism. If one of us received a special gift (other than on birthdays or Christmas), then all four of us received the same thing. If one of us received an edible treat, we were expected to share it with our sisters. Dad had one rule regarding sharing such treats: Whoever cut the treat into four pieces would receive the leftover piece after the other three sisters had chosen theirs. It was amazing how precise, accurate, and even those pieces always turned out to be! The one who made the cuts wanted to be sure to receive just as much as her sisters. It was a hoot!

Although all of these accounts of land divisions may seem boring to us, they are extremely important to the Israelites. After battling long and hard, the people are witnessing firsthand the fulfillment of God's promises to Abraham—that his descendants will inherit the land on which they now stand.

**Read Joshua 18:1–10. What stands out to you in those passages?**

With the land finally at rest, Joshua gathers the people at the tent of meeting. The land inheritance had already been set for the eastern tribes, Caleb, Judah, Ephraim, and Manasseh. It is now time to parcel out the remaining seven western tribes.

**According to Joshua 18:10, how were the land allotments determined?**

As we learned earlier in our study, the land allotments were parceled out through the casting of lots, whereas the Israelites' inheritance of the Promised Land as a whole was a promised gift from God.

## Tribal Allotments for Benjamin

**What does Genesis 49:27 reveal about the tribe of Benjamin?**

**Read Joshua 18:11–28.**

Benjamin was the youngest son of Jacob and the only one of his sons born in the Promised Land (Genesis 35:16–21).

There are a few interesting details about the land that the tribe of Benjamin is allotted. They receive one of the smallest land allotments. However, the location is very strategic as it includes roadways that merchants used, which brought wealth and commerce to the area.

Also, Benjamin's allotment includes Jericho and Jerusalem. To this day, Jericho's date trees produce dates that are world-renowned. I never leave Jericho without purchasing a few pounds of those delicious fruits to share.

## Tribal Allotments for Simeon

**What does Genesis 49:5–7 reveal about the tribe of Simeon?**

**Read Joshua 19:1–9. Which tribe shares a portion of their inheritance with Simeon?**

Since Simeon's land allotment is contained within Judah's land, no border specifics are provided for Simeon's land. An interesting fact about Simeon's allotment is that it is an extremely dry area. This arid region receives only about ten inches of rain each year. Simeon's tribe is likely made up of shepherds rather than farmers.

**If you had a choice, would you prefer to be a shepherd (raising and caring for animals) or a farmer (planting and caring for the land)? Why?**

### Tribal Allotments for Zebulun

**What does Genesis 49:13 reveal about the tribe of Zebulun?**

**Read Joshua 19:10–16. How many cities does the tribe of Zebulun inherit?**

It is important to note that the Bethlehem mentioned here is Beth Lahm, which lies east of Mount Carmel. This location is not to be confused with Bethlehem in Judah, the birthplace of Jesus.

### Tribal Allotments for Issachar

**What does Genesis 49:14–15 reveal about the tribe of Issachar?**

**Read Joshua 19:17–23. How many cities does the tribe of Issachar inherit?**

## Tribal Allotments for Asher

**What does Genesis 49:20 reveal about the tribe of Asher?**

**Read Joshua 19:24–31. How many cities does the tribe of Asher inherit?**

Asher's land allotment includes the coastal plains of the Promised Land. Its rich soil is perfect for growing lush crops. Boasting a natural harbor along the Gulf of Acco (north of Mount Carmel), both its location and rich soil make Asher's allotment an important center for commerce and trade. No wonder Asher's name means "blessed" or "happy."

## Tribal Allotments for Naphtali

**What does Genesis 49:21 reveal about the tribe of Naphtali?**

Scholars say this about Naphtali's blessing:

> That blessing may indicate that this tribe, which is sent off to the north, will bound gracefully and give rise to the faithful proclamation of the Word of God. The Galilean ministry of Jesus often brought him to the area of Naphtali and its cities, which in the [New Testament] era included Capernaum, Korazin, Bethsaida, and Tiberias.[21]

**Read Joshua 19:32–39. How many cities does the tribe of Naphtali inherit?**

Naphtali's tribal allotment is long and narrow. Significantly, it includes the western shores of the Sea of Galilee. To this day, the land is some of the most beautiful and fertile in all of Israel.

An interesting archaeological note is that Rakkath was located near the Sea of Galilee. Some evidence has been uncovered revealing that the city of Tiberias was later built on the site of Rakkath's ruins.

### Tribal Allotments for Dan

**What does Genesis 49:16–18 reveal about the tribe of Dan?**

**Read Joshua 19:40–48. How many cities does the tribe of Dan inherit?**

The Aijalon mentioned in verse 42 is the valley where Joshua uttered his audacious, faith-filled request to God: "Sun, stand still at Gibeon, and moon, in the Valley of Aijalon" (Joshua 10:12).

You did it! That may have felt very tedious, so congratulations on hanging in there. The varied topography, use of each allotted land, and special nuances of each work together to display the fact that no detail goes unnoticed by God. He could have simply instructed Joshua to allot the land based on the rock-paper-scissors method. Yet He specifically chooses each land for each particular tribe.

### Tribal Allotments for Joshua

Last, but certainly not least, we arrive at the tribal allotment for Moses' successor and Israel's great leader, Joshua. Like Caleb, Joshua receives a special inheritance apart from the tribal allotments. Our modern mindset may reason that he deserves the biggest and best portion of the Promised Land, right?

**Read Joshua 19:49–51. What city does Joshua specifically request from the Lord?**

Before verse 50, there is no biblical record of Joshua requesting the city of Timnath-serah in the hill country near Ephraim.

> The Hebrew is ambiguous as to whether the LORD commanded Israel to give Joshua whatever city he should request, or whether the LORD commanded Israel specifically to give Joshua Timnath-serah. In either case, there is no earlier passage that records such a divine command.[22]

However, Joshua was from the tribe of Ephraim. Like Caleb, Joshua chooses land within the boundaries of another tribe's inheritance. As Moses' spy, Joshua had been chosen to represent Ephraim. Perhaps Joshua just wants to call the place of his ancestors home.

Even at eighty-five years old, Joshua still has the strength and fortitude to build up the city in which he chose to live. It is also the place where Joshua would be buried. Joshua's tomb is one of the most striking monuments in Israel.

The land allotments are now complete for the twelve tribes of Israel and their leader. God gave them the land in which to establish roots, homes, and communities. What was once a pagan land of idol worshipers became a God-fearing land of Yahweh worshipers.

**How do you appreciate and leverage the allotment God has given to you?**

God has strategically placed you in the homes, communities, and churches where you do life.

**With the strength and fortitude of the living God, how will you strategically lift His name high?**

## GO QUIET, GO DEEP

Quiet your mind from distractions and pull your Bible close. Bow your head and ask Jesus to make His Word and today's text personal for you.

Take your time writing out Deuteronomy 32:3–4.

What does it mean to you to proclaim the name of the Lord?

I pray that the home the Lord has allotted to you is a place of peace, rest, and ever-increasing spiritual growth.

LESSON 7

# Cities of Refuge and Israel's Inheritance

*(Joshua 20–22)*

The faithful judgment of the Lord, along with His abounding grace, shines beautifully through these chapters of Joshua.

He instructs Joshua to designate six cities of refuge as safe havens as they await trail for His people who have killed another. This offers a beautiful display of the Lord's justice and mercy. We also see how God scatters His priestly tribe throughout the Promised Land to ensure that His Word remains easily accessible to all of His people. It provides a glimpse into how His church is scattered strategically throughout the world to offer people a place to worship the Lord, serve Him, and study His Word together.

As you walk through these chapters, keep your eyes open to how God is faithful to provide places to gather in His name and keep His name central in all that we do.

DAY 1: Cities of Refuge (Joshua 20)

DAY 2: Cities of Pasturelands Allotted to Levi (Joshua 21:1–42)

DAY 3: God Kept His Promises (Joshua 21:43–45)

DAY 4: The Eastern Tribes Return Home (Joshua 22:1–9)

DAY 5: The Altar of Witness (Joshua 22:10–34)

## Key Questions:

- How do you see the grace of God in the portioning of cities of refuge?
- How have you seen God faithful to the Israelites as they inherit their land?
- Have you stood by a family member or friend as he or she fought through life's difficulties?
- How did God bless you for your faithfulness to that person?

## Day 1

# CITIES OF REFUGE

*(Joshua 20)*

The land allotments have been divided. God's people have begun dispersing to their areas of inheritance. Each clan within each tribe has scattered to fill their portion of that tribe's inheritance.

Imagine the work that needed to be done for each tribe to settle into their lands. If someone chose a city that the Israelites had burned during the conquest, for example, much cleaning and rebuilding would need to be done. If you have ever moved into a new home, that experience provides a small window into some of the settling processes that face God's people in their respective places.

Settling into new cities and new homes would also mean that the people may disagree about a wide variety of things. Even though the land had been cleansed of enemies, the people had not been cleansed from their sinful natures. What would happen if one person killed another? God has a solution: cities of refuge.

**Read Joshua 20:1–6. What stands out to you in those verses?**

The cities of refuge are appointed by God, who gave specific rules about what is to happen at the city gate and inside the city until a person who had killed someone else has been given a fair trial. In addition to such offenders, these cities offer asylum to foreigners.

All the cities of refuge had been allotted to the Levites, the priestly tribe of God's people. The spiritual ramifications are powerful. To run to a city of refuge was to run to a place where God dwelled. Yes, God can dwell anywhere. But in today's terms, it would be equivalent to seeking refuge in a church rather than a courthouse.

**When you find yourself in trying circumstances, to whom do you turn? Why?**

The default answer for Christians is that we turn to the Lord. However, if we are honest, how many of us run to our bank accounts first? to our pantries? to those around us?

Within these cities of refuge, the Levites would act as judges to determine if the death was intentional or accidental. If the death was unintentional, the man who had killed another could live safely in the city of refuge until the high priest in office at the time of the trial had died. After that time, the man could return to the town where he lived.

**Read Joshua 20:7–9.**

Take a moment to list the cities of refuge, their locations, and which tribal allotment they fell within. The first one has been done for you.

| City of Refuge | Location | Tribe |
|---|---|---|
| Kedesh | Galilee's hill country | Naphtali |
| | | |
| | | |
| | | |
| | | |
| | | |

These six cities were strategically spread out so it would not be an arduous journey for someone to reach the closest city. God establishes these cities of refuge throughout the Promised Land so that justice, rather than personal revenge, is carried out.

These cities of refuge provide a beautiful display of God's grace without diminishing God's Law. Each of these cities throughout the Promised Land demonstrates how God provides for His people, who desperately need His grace and mercy when they mess up.

**When in your life have you made the biggest mistake and needed the biggest demonstration of God's mercy and grace? What happened?**

**How did that time impact your spiritual growth?**

The cities of refuge can be seen as a foreshadowing of God's plan for our salvation through Jesus Christ. Through His death on the cross, Jesus offers us protection from eternal death and separation from God if we confess our sins and take refuge in Him.

What do the following verses say about God, our refuge?

**Psalm 46:1–3**

**2 Samuel 22:2–3**

**Psalm 7:1**

Because of the love, grace, and forgiveness of Jesus, we can face tomorrow—whatever it holds.

These cities of refuge are not provided as an escape from justice. There are two key concepts in Joshua 20:3: *accidentally* and *unintentionally*. Also, Joshua 20:5 specifies it as *without malice aforethought*. In other words, accidents happen. If you were working on top of a roof and something rolled off, accidentally killing someone below, it would be an inadvertent death without malice.

Intentionality makes all the difference. That includes our intentional sins today. That is what is referred to as "*malice aforethought*."

**What does Numbers 15:30–31 tell us?**

The Hebrew word translated as "with a high hand" literally means "with hands raised in rebellion against God."

By God's grace, Jesus' sacrifice on the cross covers even flagrant sins, like rebellion against God and His commands. Repentance and confession make all the difference.

It is important to note that those seeking refuge are still required to stand trial. These cities of refuge are not filled with murderers exempt from facing trial or consequences. They are merely safe havens from retaliation until the accused could have a fair trial. God is just, and there are consequences for sin. Those consequences do not affect our salvation, but they certainly do not feel very good.

Even at the beginning of mankind's time on earth, God made it clear that human life is to be valued. From the time of Cain killing Abel to today, God tells us, "You shall not kill." In fact, He would require a "life for a life" (Deuteronomy 19:21).

Other than in Joshua 20, the cities of refuge are also discussed in Exodus 21, Deuteronomy 19, and Numbers 35.

**Write out Exodus 21:12–13.**

**Read Numbers 35:9–34. What stands out to you in those verses?**

The person referred to as the "avenger of blood" does not have the authority to seek private vengeance. Those avengers had a legal standing in society to carry out specific judgments. So those fleeing from those judgments could await trial in a city of refuge. However, if that person left the safe boundaries of the city, the avenger of blood could legally kill him or her.

Jewish tradition holds that the roads leading to cities of refuge were always kept in pristine condition with well-marked signs and messengers stationed along the route to guide fugitives to the cities.[23]

As refugees awaited trial, they were safe only as long as they remained in the city or until the high priest died. Since the high priest was the judge, if he died, all refugees would be set free to return to their homes. His death signaled the end of a statute of limitations that ended their exile. Imagine that day of freedom!

Out of His great love for us, God provided the ultimate city of refuge for His people. As Christians, our ultimate refuge is Jesus Christ. No matter how badly we have messed up, we can never out-sin or outrun the grace and love of Christ.

He invites us to run *to* Him:

**Galatians 4:6**

**Ephesians 3:17**

**Psalm 27:8**

We have a high priest in Jesus Christ, who dramatically fulfilled our atonement and redemption on the cross. His death settled our sin debt for all eternity. What a day of freedom! Is it any wonder why we call Good Friday good?

As the forgiven and redeemed, every Christian's role is to actively serve as signposts and proclaimers to direct people to the safety and refuge of Christ.

Even the guiltiest sinner is welcomed by Christ into His saving grace. He is closer than any city of refuge. We do not have to run miles to reach Him. We simply drop to our knees.

Amazing grace—how sweet the sound (*LSB* 744:1).

## GO QUIET, GO DEEP

Quiet your mind from distractions and pull your Bible close. Bow your head and ask Jesus to make His Word and today's text personal for you.

Take your time writing out Psalm 71:3.

What does it mean to you that Jesus is your ultimate place of refuge?

I pray that no matter what happens in your life or how far you think you may be from the grace of God, you continue to run to Him as your ultimate place of refuge and redemption.

## Day 2

# CITIES OF PASTURELANDS ALLOTTED TO LEVI

*(Joshua 21:1–42)*

At long last, after the rest of the tribes had received their allotments, Joshua 21 describes the unique allotment of the tribe of Levi.

The Levites do not have any physical land inheritance because the Lord Himself is their inheritance. God does not give the Levites the land; He gives them the lordship of the land in that they are the people's spiritual leaders. The other eleven tribes give the Levites a total of forty-eight cities (including the six cities of refuge) within their lands and support them with food from the sacrificial offerings.

God's brilliant plan spreads the Levites (and their work for the Lord) across the land rather than gathering them in only one area. It is a beautiful picture of the church today. The Levites carry out worship and teaching of the Law throughout the Promised Land. They keep God's work alive among them all.

**Read Joshua 21:1–8. What stands out to you in these verses?**

Take a moment to list the number of cities allotted, the Levitical clan who receives them, and which tribal area those cities fall under. The first one has been done for you.

| Number of Cities | Levitical Clan | Tribe |
|---|---|---|
| 13 | Kohathites | Judah, Simeon, Benjamin |
| | | |
| | | |
| | | |
| | | |
| | | |

These forty-eight cities are strategically spread out so that God's people would not have to go far to gather and worship the Lord.

The Levites are uniquely blessed to spend their days teaching the Law and worshiping the Lord throughout the land. The translation of that truth in our culture today is we go into the whole earth to spread the Good News. Those who are called into full-time ministry uniquely understand this application.

**According to 1 Chronicles 23:28–32, what is the role of the Levites?**

According to the following verses, why is the tribe of Levi not granted a self-contained territorial allotment like the other tribes?

**Numbers 18:20**

**Deuteronomy 18:1–2**

**Joshua 13:33**

The Levites remind me of an Olympic team. They are scattered throughout all of Israel yet work as a team from the same playbook: God's Word. Even with vast distances between them, they need to work together for the spiritual well-being of God's people.

**Read Joshua 21:9–42.**

Did you notice that every tribe contains Levitical towns? If you look at maps from that time, many of the Levitical towns are strategically placed along land borders.

For example, the Levitical towns of Jahaz, Kedemoth, and Mephaath within the tribe of Reuben are gathered along their eastern border. Jattir and Ashan are situated along the northern border of the Negev.

**Why do you believe the Levitical towns fall along land borders?**

They are placed almost like spiritual buffers against pagan influence or like spiritual gatekeepers for anyone who enters the land.

You and I can relate to spiritual buffers in the form of Christian friends. They know us best, which means they know our sinful tendencies and the unique gifts God has given us.

**Who are the spiritual buffers God has given to you?**

I am thankful that God has graciously provided some very dear sisters and brothers in Christ who hold me accountable in various aspects of my life.

We all need God's spiritual buffers so we can live wise, discerning lives as we serve Him. First and foremost, God has given us the Holy Spirit—the ultimate spiritual buffer—who lives inside us. The Spirit dwells within us (John 14:16–17), enables us to share the Gospel (Acts 1:8; 1 Corinthians 2:1–5), and empowers us to put to death the works of the flesh (Romans 8:13; Galatians 5:16).

Both by birth and God's blessing, the Levites (descended from Aaron the high priest) have been given the special privilege to serve God in His church.

**What does Deuteronomy 33:10–11 say about the Levites?**

Despite being scattered throughout the land, the Levites serve God as a team. Pastors serve in that role today for the spiritual formation and well-being of the church as a whole and also for individuals within the church.

**How do you see this in your community or denomination?**

It is important to note that these Levitical towns are not sequestered, monastic-type places. They are strategically placed so they can serve their local communities as well as the cities around them.

Take a moment to list the names of Levitical cities given in Joshua 21:

| Scripture | Levitical Clan | Cities Given |
| --- | --- | --- |
| Joshua 21:9–19 | | |
| Joshua 21:20–26 | | |
| Joshua 21:27–33 | | |
| Joshua 21:34–40 | | |

**Take a moment to write out the concise summary from Joshua 21:41–42.**

Each of the Levitical cities has pasturelands around it. The priests could cultivate crops and herds, which would care for the physical needs of God's people. What a beautiful pairing with the Levites' role to care for their spiritual needs!

It is important to note that, although these forty-eight towns are designated as Levitical cities, not all of them served that purpose in Joshua's time.

**What do you believe the Levitical scattering accomplishes?**

It is striking how God leaves nothing to chance when it comes to the spiritual well-being of His people. No one is left out. Every Israelite has access to a nearby priest who is well-versed in the Law of Moses. The priest can provide necessary counsel and godly advice in all areas of life.

You and I have abundant access to God's church in our day and age. Even if a congregation is not physically near you or you are unable to physically attend, there are literally thousands of churches that hold online services each week, and pastors are available to make visits to people at home or in a facility to administer the Lord's Supper.

Like the Israelites in Joshua's day, it is incumbent on believers to make a concerted effort to be an active part of the local church and God's church at large. My ministry of writing, speaking, and teaching demands much travel, so I look forward to those Sundays when I can sit in my home church for worship. Attending church (in person or online) is not simply an item on a checklist. Participating in the worship service provides the extraordinary opportunity to receive God's Word and Sacraments and be part of the vibrant, beautiful body of Christ.

## GO QUIET, GO DEEP

Quiet your mind from distractions and pull your Bible close. Bow your head and ask Jesus to make His Word and today's text personal for you.

Take your time writing out Ephesians 4:11–13.

What does it mean to you to be part of a vibrant Christian community?

I pray that you continue to diligently serve the Lord in active, joyful service in your local church and community.

## DAY 3

# GOD KEPT HIS PROMISES

*(Joshua 21:43–45)*

As I write this day's session, my sisters and I are in the process of moving my mom in to live with me. It is a significant life change to put it mildly. Perhaps you have been there, done that, and have the T-shirt.

I feel as if I am saying goodbye to many blessings that, until now, I have taken for granted. Like uninterrupted quiet time. Not having to explain where I am going or how I spend my time. A relaxed routine.

Mom will experience similar changes as well. It's not just about me and my selfish preferences. It's about ensuring a high quality of life for Mom in her twilight years surrounded by family instead of living alone.

I have come to realize that God is simply replacing my blessings with different ones. Uninterrupted time deepening the loving relationship we already enjoy. Planning fun outings together since she does not drive anymore. A routine of healthy habits for both of our sakes.

Change is hard, isn't it? This change has made me realize that our attitude toward change matters. Embracing change requires a forward-looking attitude. It actively looks for God in ways we have not experienced before. Change forces us to look for joy in the unfamiliar.

Through many centuries and much heartache and blessing, God's people are now settled in the Promised Land. They are not saying goodbye to many blessings; rather, they are embracing many new ones from the Lord. God has changed their home from the desert to the Promised Land. For the young generation of Israelites whom God has brought into Canaan, they have only known the hard life of the desert before crossing the Jordan. They have known years of warfare and bloodshed. They have known tent-living and a nomadic lifestyle. Now, to be at peace and rest in the Promised Land is the culmination of their entire life's journey. They have followed the Lord to a home and land for their families to call their own.

Today's text consists of only three verses. However, these verses summarize the culmination of God's promise to His people through Abraham in Genesis 12 (when he was known as Abram).

**Read and write out Joshua 21:43.**

This verse demonstrates that God was faithful to all of the promises that He made to Joshua seven years earlier in Joshua 1.

**Reread Joshua 1:2–9. What did God promise to Joshua that you see has now come to pass?**

God promised that "every place that the sole of your foot will tread upon I have given to you" (Joshua 1:3). Now Joshua and all of God's people stand in the physical reality of God's promise. Joshua prayed, trusted the Lord, and moved in obedience.

Standing in the reality of answered prayer offers a grand view of the faithfulness and grace of God. When I started writing and teaching God's Word almost twenty years ago, my ongoing prayer was that one day God would arrange my work life so I could do this work full time. Today, my feet are standing in the physical reality of God's faithfulness to bring that prayer to fruition. It is a humbling reality that sends fireworks through my soul! My days are now filled with studying God's Word, writing Bible studies, and traveling the world to teach them.

**Are you living in the reality of the prayers you once prayed? If so, how?**

**How has it affected your relationship with the Lord?**

God inspires the best dreams because the best dreams honor Him. The best dreams use the gifts that He has specifically given you to use for His glory. And He who promised is faithful to bring it all to fruition.

What do the following verses say about God's faithfulness?

**Psalm 36:5**

**1 Corinthians 1:9**

**Lamentations 3:22–23**

The Promised Land is not fully occupied until the time of David and Solomon. Then again under Uzziah and Jeroboam. In Joshua 21:45, the precise boundaries that stretch from Mount Hermon to the Negeb and from the Mediterranean Sea to the Arabian Desert will be set.

**Read and write out Joshua 21:44.**

God's people had just endured seven years of violence and warfare. Seven years of the adrenaline and fight-or-flight mode that war demands.

The medical community has done much research on the fight-or-flight response when the human body encounters life-and-death situations. These are some of the physical signs when danger threatens:

1. *Dilated pupils.* The body becomes more aware of its surroundings. Dilated pupils allow more light into the eyes for better vision.
2. *Pale or flushed skin.* The skin color alters as blood rushes to the head and brain.

3. *Blood clotting.* The body increases its ability for the blood to clot to prevent excess blood loss in case of injury.
4. *Rapid heart rate and breathing.* These provide the body with the energy and oxygen needed to fuel rapid response to danger.
5. *Trembling.* Muscles tense and become primed for action, which can cause trembling or shaking.

There are benefits to the fight-or-flight mode. It primes the body for action, creates physical stress so the body can handle pressure better and remain alert, and plays a critical role in survival to protect and preserve the body from harm.

**If you have ever lived in a state of fight-or-flight mode for an extended amount of time, how did it affect you spiritually and physically?**

We will never fully know the extraordinary capabilities of our physical bodies that God created and gifted to us.

The psychological drawback of the fight-or-flight mode is that it can be triggered by both real and imaginary threats. Even our phobias, like a fear of public speaking, heights, spiders, and so on, can falsely trigger it. Those false triggers can be harmful to physical health through chronic fatigue, depression, gastrointestinal issues, headaches and migraines, heart attacks, and high blood pressure.

Taking all of that into consideration, can you imagine how completely exhausted God's people are after seven years of warfare and battling the fight-or-flight response? They were in enemy territory, so even when they were not on the offense in battle, they were constantly on alert for surprise attacks. Joshua 21:44 confirms that the Lord now gave them rest on every side. They could exhale and sleep with both eyes closed.

The vast majority of us today do not engage in the physical combat of war, but we are engaged daily in spiritual warfare. Thankfully, our rest is found through faith in our Lord and Savior. Jesus alone gives us lasting rest.

**Read Hebrews 4:8–9.**

Israel had faithfully obeyed the Lord under Joshua's leadership, so God gave them complete victory over their enemies and rest from war.

**Write out Joshua 21:45.**

Regardless of how often you and I fail our God-given tasks, God's grace and mercy prevail. God kept His promises to Joshua. God kept His promise to the Israelites. And God keeps His promises to us because they are based on His fidelity, not ours.

**What does 2 Timothy 2:13 tell us?**

Our unfaithfulness never changes God's faithfulness.

Like He gave to the Israelites, the Lord has faithfully given us rest over our enemies. Christ won on the cross the victory over sin and death for all time for all who believe by faith. Grace!

## GO QUIET, GO DEEP

Quiet your mind from distractions and pull your Bible close. Bow your head and ask Jesus to make His Word and today's text personal for you.

Take your time writing out Deuteronomy 7:9.

What does it mean to you that God is faithful to you?

I pray that as God is faithful to you, you share His faithful love and message of salvation to all whom He puts in your path.

## Day 4

# THE EASTERN TRIBES RETURN HOME

*(Joshua 22:1–9)*

Our incredible journey through the book of Joshua has seen Joshua and the Israelites enter the land, conquer the land, and divide the land. Under the leadership of Joshua, all twelve tribes worked as a team, with God as their Commander, to get to this point.

Over the better part of seven years, the tribes allotted land on the east side of the Jordan had stood beside their brothers and sisters to conquer Canaan. These eastern tribes had sacrificed themselves and time with their families to stand shoulder-to-shoulder with their fellow Israelites to conquer land for the western tribes that they would not personally possess.

After years of fighting, the eastern tribes are now free to return home. It is time for the western tribes to bid farewell to some of their comrades in arms.

**Read Joshua 22:1–5. What stands out to you in those verses?**

After seven years of faithful service and honoring their commitment, Joshua releases the Reubenites, Gadites, and half-tribe of Manasseh from duty to return to their land allotments east of the Jordan River.

He praises their commitment and loyalty to keeping the charge. They have fought as faithful and valiant warriors. Joshua realizes that they will be separated geographically from the rest of the Israelites, so he takes time to impart four specific commands before they depart: (1) observe the Lord's commandments, (2) love the Lord, (3) walk in the Lord's ways, and (4) serve the Lord with all of their heart and soul (Joshua 22:5).

### Observe the Lord's commandments

This is reminiscent of a parent sending his or her child to college. For the first time, parent and child will be separated significantly by geography and a parent's watchful gaze. Those parents pray their children will not fall away from faith and will continue to observe the Lord's commands.

It is reminiscent of Paul's letters to the church at Corinth who fell into arguments and sin after Paul's departure.

Although God may seem far away, the truth is that He lives inside us through the power of the Holy Spirit. We are never without God's watchful care and keeping.

Joshua reminds them to stay alert ("be very careful") because distance from the tabernacle might lead to distance from God.

For me, Joshua's reminder brought to mind the 2020 COVID-19 pandemic. As church doors closed, we scrambled to stay connected. We gravitated toward Zoom and online streaming and went above and beyond to find ways to stay connected with each other as the Body of Christ.

**What new and innovative ways did you use to stay connected during the pandemic? What did you learn along the way?**

Joshua reminds the Israelites to be very careful to stay connected to the Lord and each other.

### Love the Lord

Formerly surrounded by a pagan culture that carved and loved idols, Joshua reminds them to love the Lord above all else. The Hebrew word used here is used in the context of loving the Lord only one other time in Scripture (Joshua 23:11). Joshua does not ask the Israelites to love an unknown god but to love Yahweh, who has kept His promise to see them safely through to the land of their inheritance. Israel can love God because the evidence of His faithfulness surrounds them.

That wise advice is relevant for every believer. Our culture loosely uses the word *love*, but here Joshua says there is one to love above all: the Lord

God Almighty. He has done marvelous things and is worthy to receive the love of His people.

Write out the following verses about the love of God:

**Romans 5:8**

**1 John 4:16**

**1 John 3:1**

**Jeremiah 31:3**

**Where in your life right now do you need these reminders of God's love for you?**

God's love for us surpasses all time, space, and barriers. Loving Him—even when we do not understand our circumstances—keeps our eyes on Him and His mighty works.

> Covenant faithfulness, Joshua impresses, does not consist of mere outward obedience. Love for the LORD, who loved Israel first and by the grace established his covenant love with her, is the very heart of faithfulness. The first and greatest commandment was given through Moses and was repeated by the One to

> whom Moses and all the prophets testify: "Love the LORD your God with all your heart and with all your soul and with all your strength" ([Deuteronomy] 6:5 . . .).[24]

### WALK IN THE LORD'S WAYS

Under Joshua's leadership and the unity of their fellow Israelites, God's people had walked in the Lord's ways. Throughout Scripture, the Lord's relationship with His people is depicted as a marriage. A covenant relationship.

However, Joshua knows that man's sinful nature is still at play while His people walk the earth. God promised the eastern tribes much wealth and livestock, so it would be easy to rely on self and treasures seen rather than on God and spiritual treasures unseen.

What do the following verses say about walking in the Lord's ways?

**1 John 2:6**

**Galatians 5:25**

Walking in the ways of the Lord honors Jesus' sacrifice and paves the way to eternity for all who believe. During hard seasons of life, walking in the Lord's ways and trusting that He will get us through makes all the difference in the world.

### SERVE THE LORD WITH ALL OF THEIR HEART AND SOUL

Joshua provides a bookend in his final words to the eastern tribes before they depart. Everything the eastern tribes said they would do in Joshua 1:12–18, they have now done. Joshua honors their service by recognizing their faithfulness.

**How do you currently serve the Lord with all of your heart and soul?**

**What impact has your service made on your spiritual journey or the lives of others?**

After commending them for their faithful service and reminding them to continue to serve the Lord, Joshua blesses them as they head eastward back home. However, Joshua ensures that the tribe of Reuben, Gad, and the half-tribe of Manasseh did not return home empty-handed.

**Read Joshua 22:6–9. What stands out to you in these verses?**

Just in case the other nine and one-half tribes forgot, Joshua specifically reminds them to divide the significant spoils gained from their enemies with their brethren.

Greed can easily turn a man's heart away from the Lord. We saw that example in the life of Achan following the destruction of Jericho. Though Achan attempted to hide his sin, his greed cost the lives of thirty-six Israelites, his family, and himself.

All God's people were settling in new lands—some in areas destroyed or damaged during their conquest. There was much work to do in the cities and land. They would need money for homes, to plant crops, to raise livestock, to care for their families, and to set up defensive manpower in each place. All that takes wealth.

**What does John 4:36 tell us?**

The overarching message from Joshua to the eastern tribes acknowledges their faithful service to God but also calls on them to continue their faithful services.

This lesson still rings true today for God's people in their families, work places, and witness around the world.

## GO QUIET, GO DEEP

Quiet your mind from distractions and pull your Bible close. Bow your head and ask Jesus to make His Word and today's text personal for you.

Take your time writing out Zephaniah 3:17.

What does it mean to you that God rejoices over you with singing and loves you unconditionally?

I pray that as God has loved you unconditionally, you unconditionally love the people God puts in your life.

## Day 5

# THE ALTAR OF WITNESS

*(Joshua 22:10–34)*

Have you ever done anything with the purest of motives only for it to be so grossly misunderstood that arguments and issues arose?

This is where we find ourselves in Joshua chapter 22. Joshua releases the eastern tribes to return to their land. Their western brethren divide their spoils of war and part ways from their former comrades in arms. A misunderstanding arises, gossip leads to dissension, and suddenly their thoughts turn toward declaring war on each other.

**Read Joshua 22:10–12. What did the eastern tribes build?**

On their way home, when the Reubenites, Gadites, and half-tribe of Manasseh reach the Jordan, they build an altar in praise and honor to the Lord. In fact, it is "an altar of imposing size." Word gets back to the people of Israel on the western side. They "heard it said" (gossip, not fact) that they are building a competing altar, not a symbolic one. The western tribes had set up the altar at Shiloh, so they wrongly assume the eastern tribes set up their own altar to be more geographically convenient.

**What does Deuteronomy 12:13–14 say?**

In their eyes, the western tribes believe that the altar built by the eastern tribes is a direct violation of God's command. Their reaction may seem extreme, but the Israelites (thanks to their wilderness wanderings) fully understand the danger of unfaithfulness to God. They believe that if the eastern tribes built an altar (in the traditional sense), then their nation is in trouble.

There are valuable lessons here—both positive and negative—that we cannot miss. It was commendable that the western tribes desired to faithfully adhere to God's Law. However, their knee-jerk reaction based on assumption was a definite negative.

**Have you seen this scenario play out in your church or the church at large? If so, what was the result?**

Knee-jerk reactions are more often than not based on emotions rather than facts. There is a personal affront or corporate fear, and the scene deteriorates from there.

**Read Joshua 22:13–20. What stands out to you in these verses?**

Thankfully, the western tribes choose to send a delegation to the eastern tribes to ascertain their intentions rather than show up with drawn swords. However, when the western tribes reach the eastern tribes, their first words contain judgment. In Joshua 22:12, the western tribes were "the people of Israel." In Joshua 22:16, they became "the whole congregation of the LORD." In effect, the western tribes have already verbally excommunicated the eastern tribes from the Body of God's people. But the judgmentalism does not stop there.

What questions do the western tribes ask the eastern tribes?

**Joshua 22:16**

**Joshua 22:17–18**

**Joshua 22:20**

Ouch! Even though the western tribes have approached the eastern tribes to discover the facts regarding their altar, their demand for explanation is fueled by aggressive, rhetorical questions. This could turn ugly fast.

**Read Joshua 22:21–29. Write a short summary of how the eastern tribes respond.**

What a humble and gracious response! Rather than offering a hostile, defensive response that could have only made matters worse, they invoke God's name (in fact, three divine names: *El, Elohim,* and *Yahweh*) and patiently explain their reason for building the altar.

Rather than answer the western tribes' questions, they cut straight to the heart of the matter and explain their motive. The eastern tribes are mortified to learn that the altar they built for the Lord was perceived as rebellion by their western brothers. In effect, they say, "If our motive is wrong, then strike us down."

**If you have ever been wrongly accused, how did you respond?**

Cutting to the heart of the matter to discern fact from assumption is a great place to start.

Let's pause to address an important question. Wouldn't a replica of the Lord's altar be considered an idol? After all, they had just conquered a land that worshiped idols. However, an altar is just a structure unless it is used for worship. The eastern tribes never intended to worship God at that altar. Therefore, it is simply a fancy ebenezer.

There is another clue that the western tribes should have noticed. The eastern tribes built the altar on the *western* side of the Jordan. It was an inconvenient and impractical location for regular sacrifices—especially during spring floods. Their altar served as a physical reminder for the eastern tribes *to cross the Jordan* in order to worship God as one nation.

**Read Joshua 22:30–34.**

Despite the assumption of guilt and hostile questions posed by the western tribes, there are three positive characteristics to acknowledge.

First, it is *personal*. The western tribes could easily marshal forces and march against the eastern tribes. Instead, they send a delegation headed by a priest to express their concerns before picking a fight. That is an admirable way to approach it.

Second, it is *passionate*. The western tribes are concerned about the spiritual condition of the eastern tribes and their faithfulness to God. They attempt to turn the eastern tribes from what they consider to be sin. So we give them credit for a pure motive, even if their approach is faulty.

Third, it is *purposeful*. The western tribes' actions show their desire to remain one nation in their commitment to God, even though the Jordan River separates them.

The situation ends peaceably after the misunderstanding is cleared up. However, it is instructive to believers today to follow Jesus' teaching in Matthew 18 to go directly to the source of the issue rather than stir the gossip pot.

**Read and summarize Matthew 18:15–17.**

To the credit of the western tribes, they recognize and acknowledge that their knee-jerk reaction caused them to jump to the wrong conclusions about the motives of the eastern tribes. They return to harmonious fellowship and the conflict is never again mentioned in Scripture.

**In Joshua 22:34, what do the eastern tribes call their altar?**

The strongest witness for the Lord is love toward one another. Jesus teaches His disciples (and us today) this powerful truth.

Write out the following verses:

**John 13:34–35**

**John 15:12–13**

**Have you ever jumped to the wrong conclusion about someone else's motives? If so, what happened?**

**What spiritual lessons did the Lord give you through that experience?**

It is a beautiful example of God's grace at work in our life for Christ-followers to freely admit when we are in the wrong and be the first to move toward reconciliation.

There is much to be said for community among God's people who are determined to stay together through thick and thin.

Honest and open communication, along with refraining from knee-jerk reactions and gossip, is crucial.

## GO QUIET, GO DEEP

Quiet your mind from distractions and pull your Bible close. Bow your head and ask Jesus to make His Word and today's text personal for you.

Take your time writing out Proverbs 15:14.

What does it mean to you to patiently discern the motives of others without jumping to conclusions?

I pray that the Golden Rule of "Do unto others as you would have them do unto you" guides your daily interactions.

## LESSON 8

# JOSHUA FINISHES WELL

*Joshua 23–24*

The Israelites spent seven years conquering the land and thirteen years occupying it. Twenty years after God's people crossed the raging Jordan, we arrive at the end of the book of Joshua. The people have changed significantly. They went from nomads to conquerors. Wanderers to workers. Warriors to worshipers. All taking place in the physical reality of God's promises to Abraham.

The lessons learned from the Israelites' journey can easily apply to our Christian walk today. God's plan for each of our lives in Christ Jesus takes many years to come to fruition through battles, facing opposition, and trusting the Lord every step of the way. As we walk through our land, we walk in the Spirit.

DAY 1: Joshua's Charge to Israel's Leaders (Joshua 23)

DAY 2: The Covenant Renewal at Shechem (Joshua 24:1–13)

DAY 3: Choose Whom You Will Serve (Joshua 24:14–28)

DAY 4: Joshua's Death and Burial (Joshua 24:29–33)

DAY 5: Remembering the Lessons from the Book of Joshua

**KEY QUESTIONS:**

- What has God asked of you, His beloved child?
- How does your life reflect that it is the Lord you serve?
- What do you want people to remember about you after you are home in heaven?

## DAY 1

# JOSHUA'S CHARGE TO ISRAEL'S LEADERS

*(Joshua 23)*

Twenty years have passed since Joshua led God's people across the raging Jordan River. It may have seemed like yesterday or a lifetime ago for God's people, but their journey has been punctuated by God's faithfulness. In his old age, Joshua prepares to hand the leadership reigns to the next generation. When Joshua dies, God will not appoint a solitary leader like Moses or Joshua. And like Moses, Joshua prepares to share parting words in three farewell sermons.

Throughout our journey through the book of Joshua, we have seen time and again how the Promised Land conquest mirrors our Christian life. We have battles to fight, enemies to evict, and ground to take. We need God-given courage to step onto the battlefield and faith to trust Him for victory.

### Remember God's Works

**Read Joshua 23:1–5. What stands out to you in these verses?**

Similar to the final speeches of Moses in Deuteronomy, Joshua begins with the fact that his time on this earth and as their leader is coming to an end. We do not know if that came as a surprise to God's people. However, Joshua is now 110 years old, and the clock is rapidly ticking down.

First and most important, Joshua reminds them how they were eyewitnesses to God's faithfulness and miraculous works. Time and settling the land may have faded their memories, but Joshua wants to ensure that God's faithfulness burns vividly in their hearts and minds. God had gone before them to secure one victory after another. Then, when all was said and done, God delivered the promised inheritance. They have now lived in peace in their own homes and cities for thirteen years.

**Take a moment to write out Joshua 23:5.**

Although God gave them resounding victory in the Promised Land, not all the Canaanites had been defeated or driven out. Here, Joshua reminds the people that there would be work ahead, but that God would fight the fight on their behalf once again.

**As you read that verse again, how has God fought for you recently?**

**Have you shared with others how your God fought for you? Why or why not?**

What does God say about fighting for you in the following verses?

**Isaiah 54:17**

**Exodus 13:14**

**Deuteronomy 20:4**

**In the battles that you face in this season of life, how do these verses bless and strengthen you?**

Sometimes our battles seem to last a lifetime. Joshua could empathize. Although Joshua conquered part of the Promised Land and began to settle God's people in Canaan, it would take generations—until King David's time—to take hold of their full inheritance.

### Hold Steadfast to God's Word

**Read Joshua 23:6–10. What stands out to you in these verses?**

Joshua employs the same phrase that the Lord Himself said to Joshua: Be strong (see Joshua 1:7–8). Joshua had led the Israelites for two decades by prioritizing unwavering obedience to God's commands. Joshua now challenges the leaders to hold that same priority. Did you notice that Joshua does not add anything? Joshua reminds them to remain steadfast to follow God and His commands wholeheartedly.

For us today, that means spending time with God. In my walk with Him, I use Bible studies to learn more about the Lord. I am so thankful to Martin Luther and the other reformers who risked life and limb to translate the Bible into modern languages. Because of their work, we can actually hold the Word of God in our hands.

**What is your normal Bible study routine?**

**Do you follow a Bible reading plan or work through Scripture at your own pace?**

**According to Joshua 23:6, what is the standard for godly living?**

It is simple: God's Word. Follow what has already been written and commanded. But you and I know that is not always as easy to do as it is to say. We often struggle as well. On busy days, time passes like lightning as we work through our impressive to-do lists. On lazy days, time slips through our fingers like water. Intentionality makes all the difference when it comes to faithfully studying God's Word.

**What else does Joshua 23:7 command?**

God's people were not to "mix" with the surrounding pagan nation in worshiping their gods. As we have learned in this study, God gave the Canaanites over six centuries to turn toward Him and worship the one true God. They refused and worshiped idols. Through Joshua, God warns the Israelites to remain steadfast to Him alone.

In such a technologically connected world, it becomes more and more challenging for believers to not mix with our culture.

**As God's child, what does it mean to you to not mix with today's culture?**

**In not mixing, how are you faithful to be God's salt and light in the world?**

The challenge is real. The ramifications are huge. Write out the following verses that shed light on this important topic:

**2 Corinthians 6:14–17**

**Romans 12:2**

**John 15:19**

It is hard to read that the world will hate you simply because you follow the One who loves everyone most. Yet God faithfully gives us the strength to endure and persevere.

Joshua's speech provides an important truth for believers in all generations: Godly living is not achieved by slam-dunking a single battle but by enlisting for lifelong service. Although the Israelites are settled in the Promised Land, many enemies still need to be conquered. As God's people settled near the Canaanites, temptation and a fascination with a pagan lifestyle could lure them away from God. It's the same in our culture today. The enemy makes many worldly things look tempting or beneficial for us, when in actuality they are a hook to drag us away from intimacy with the Lord.

**Can you identify any of those hooks present in your life right now?**

God's people face their greatest spiritual threat in the Promised Land. The blatant pagan culture around them would continually try to lure them away from God. Yet Joshua reminds them that the God who gave them victory in the desert will give them victory in Canaan.

### Remember God's Warning

**Read Joshua 23:11–16. What stands out to you in these verses?**

As any good leader knows, starting with positive reinforcement provides great motivation. However, fear also works. The consequences of not following God wholeheartedly were real.

**In Joshua 23:12–13, what does Joshua warn the Israelites?**

Joshua tells them there are three consequences if they fail to love and serve the Lord. First, they will be defeated. Second, they will experience discomfort. Finally, they will end in disgrace.

God does not instruct them to strengthen their military force or bolster their economy. Ungodly alliances and pagan intermarriage are the greatest spiritual dangers. If someone's heart is lured away, the rest of the mind and body will follow. The blessings of God fall upon all who fully devote themselves to Him in love.

God took Israel out of Egypt, but it took forty years in the desert to get Egypt out of Israel. They were free but complained about their food and accommodations in the desert. Are you and I any different? We can take the Christian out of the world but it is hard to take the world out of the Christian. We love the familiarity of family and friends and the comfort of the blessings the Lord has given us, but once we start putting any of those things before our love for the Lord, it is a steep slide into the world away from the Lord.

What do the following verses tell us about remaining steadfast in the Lord?

**James 1:12**

**1 Corinthians 15:58**

**2 Peter 3:17–18**

The common denominator in those verses is that motivation comes from inside us and not from the outside. From the beginning of the book of Joshua to the end, the clear message is to remain faithful to the Lord no matter what.

When the Lord tells you to be in the world and not of the world (see John 17:14–15), He does not mean go live in a monastery and shut yourself off from outside contact. Some Christians are determined to have only Christian friends and neighbors and not interact with unbelievers. But consider that Jesus prayed that God would not take believers out of the world but that He would keep us from the evil one while we are in the world.

**Are you intentional about interacting in the world? If so, what does that look like?**

The Israelites needed to know that the same God who rescued, protected, and abundantly blessed them could just as easily punish and destroy them if they were unfaithful.

Such power reminds me of Niagara Falls. I visited there several years ago with the production crew as we were filming a Bible study in New York. The water looks beautiful and peaceful from a distance. But when we stepped up to the edge, its fury and danger were sobering. So it is with the Lord. His love and grace flow with beauty and peace in our lives, but disobedience and rejecting the Lord's commands put us at the edge of the fury and wrath of God.

Joshua has passed the torch to the next generation of Israel's leaders whom God will raise up. Just as Moses had passed it to him.

Just as Paul passed it to the elders at Ephesus (Acts 20).

Just as the Lord has passed it to us.

This truth brings forth a reminder to those of us who are older and a bit more mature in faith. There is a new generation of young adults who need to not only hear these words but also see faithfulness to God demonstrated in how we live, serve, and interact.

**Write out Joshua 23:14.**

That is a powerful verse! It is highlighted in my Bible to remind me that the Lord has been faithful over my life even before I knew He was Lord over my life.

Everything God has said He has kept. In every promise from the times of Adam and Eve to today, God continues to be faithful.

**How have you specifically seen the promises of God take root and produce spiritual fruit in your life?**

### Conditional Blessing

God gave His people the Promised Land as an inheritance, but that inheritance came with conditions. God's covenant with Abraham was made with all conditions held up by God Himself, yet as God's people moved into their inheritance, their peace, well-being, and rest depended on the condition of following God wholeheartedly.

To be clear, salvation and redemption are solely the work of God. We do not work to earn any of God's promises. Yet as you and I have discovered, our ungodly choices and unfaithful hearts can land us in a world of spiritual hurt. In Deuteronomy 28, Moses reminded the people that if they honored God, He would bless them. If they disobeyed God, He would destroy them.

For you and me, there are consequences when we sin and stray from the Lord's commands. Although God will not destroy us, He will withhold His blessings over our lives until, by faith, He returns our hearts to His.

## GO QUIET, GO DEEP

Quiet your mind from distractions and pull your Bible close. Bow your head and ask Jesus to make His Word and today's text personal for you.

Take your time writing out Acts 20:24.

What does it mean to you to finish the ministry that the Lord has given you? To whom specifically is He preparing you to pass the torch of faith?

I pray that God keeps your heart on fire for Him and keeps you faithful to His Word.

## DAY 2

# THE COVENANT RENEWAL AT SHECHEM

*(Joshua 24:1–13)*

Much like one Olympic runner hands the baton to the next, Moses handed off the baton of leadership to Joshua. Joshua faithfully took the handoff and carried it to the point when he was nearing death. God would not designate another person to whom the baton could be passed. Israel, as a nation, would now be responsible for keeping it off the ground.

Through the guidance and strength of the Lord, Joshua led a mass of desert nomads into the land God had promised them and established them as a respected nation. Joshua was a person worth listening to. So his final words to God's people carry much significance. After all, who could follow Joshua? Under his leadership, only one battle was lost during the seven-year military campaign to conquer the Promised Land. And that loss was not even Joshua's failure but that of his greedy military personnel.

As we arrive at Joshua 24, we have marched with Joshua from the east to the west. Seven years of war and more than two decades of settling into their inheritance. We have studied how the walls fell down, the sun stood still, ebenezers were raised, and altars were built to glorify God.

At last, Israel's great leader gathers all of God's people at Shechem for his final commission and challenge to the whole population. As Joshua speaks, the Lord prepares God's people for Joshua's departure from this life into his heavenly reward.

**Read Joshua 24:1. At what city does Joshua gather all of God's people?**

Did you notice that Joshua does not start with their current situation? He takes them back to Abraham so they remember all that God provided for the patriarchs and all that He provided for Israel. The location Joshua selects to deliver his farewell speech holds rich significance for God's people.

**According to Genesis 12:6–7, what happened at Shechem?**

As Joshua addresses Abraham's offspring, perhaps Joshua even stood by Abraham's altar. Perhaps he stood near the stones on which he wrote God's Law during the people's covenant renewal in the Valley of Shechem (Joshua 8:30–35). The location served as a vivid visual reminder of all God had done for His people.

**Read Joshua 24:2–12. If you knew that you were about to die and had one last chance to speak, what would you say?**

I doubt I would have started with the words "I am old" as Joshua had in 23:2. The truth is that we don't know until that moment arrives. We do not know where we will be, who will be around us, or even when it will be. But I pray that my words will be about Jesus. Uplifting words about what He has done in my life and what He is faithful to do in the lives of all who love Him.

Joshua delivers a powerful historical review of God's salvation for His people and methodically delineates God's mighty and awesome deeds on Israel's behalf. He uses the typical Jewish pattern of storytelling. He weaves their history into their present through his historical review. In Acts 7, Stephen used the same typical pattern of storytelling.

In Joshua 24:7, Joshua reminds God's people that their eyes saw what the Lord did for them. *They saw.* It was not hearsay or gossip. They had seen and experienced firsthand what God had done for them in the desert and in the land He had given them.

As believers, testifying and witnessing to others about what we have seen is as powerful today as it was in biblical times.

How do you see the example set in the following verses?

**John 3:11**

**Acts 4:19–20**

**1 John 1:1–3**

The disciples *saw* how God worked powerfully through them. The Israelites *saw* how the Lord fought for them. In other words, their experiences were not about the *land* but the *Lord*. It was not about Moses, Joshua, or any other human being. Our witness is never about the servant but always about the Savior.

Joshua gives a master class review of Israel's covenant history, commitment, and action through the power of the Lord. Every word paints a vivid portrait of the immeasurable blessings of a covenant relationship with God. There is a curious reference in Joshua 24:12 that may leave us scratching our heads. It says, "And I sent the hornet before you, which drove them out before you." Scholars offer three possible explanations:

> 1. "The hornet" may be a colorful metaphor for the dread that gripped the Canaanites. After the LORD stung Israel's enemies with defeat, the hornet of terror winged its way to future opponents to paralyze them. . . .
>
> 2. Some commentators point out that the hornet was a symbol of Lower Egypt. They suggest that prior to Israel's conquest, excursions of Egypt's army into Canaan had weakened the Canaanites, and thus Egypt's army was "the hornet." . . .

3. A literal interpretation of "the hornet" is also possible. The same LORD who summoned frogs, gnats, flies, and locusts to plague the Egyptians (Exodus 8–10) could also gather swarms of hornets to terrorize the Canaanites and throw them into confusion before Israel joined them in battle.[25]

The bottom line is that "the hornet" did not bode well for Israel's enemies.

The three bodies of water that were milestones in Israel's journey to the Promised Land are all mentioned in Joshua 24. First is the Euphrates River, which Abraham crossed (Joshua 24:2–3). Second is the Red Sea, which Moses and God's people crossed after God parted it (Joshua 24:6). Third is the Jordan River, where Joshua and God's people crossed into the Promised Land (Joshua 24:11).

Each time God took His people across water, they entered lands where pagans and false gods reigned. God placed them in each land to have influence and make a difference in the name of the Lord. The Israelites also came *from* lands where false gods were worshiped, yet the Lord faithfully turned their hearts to Him. No one is beyond His mighty works of salvation. Like the Israelites, we have all turned from idols that had the same root: *self-centeredness.*

**Do you struggle with self-centeredness? If so, what do you do to combat those thoughts?**

Living alone and accustomed to my own schedule, I struggle with self-centeredness. I believe that the Lord will use this new season of life with Mom moving in to go a long way toward correcting it.

Our days, lives, and agendas tend to revolve around us and our pleasure. But when we step into the river of life—when we come through the water and Word in our Baptism—we see our life in the greater context of the Body of believers who will spend eternity with God. We can turn our gaze away from our inward lives and look outward to the kingdom of God.

People have debated for centuries over who owns the land of Israel. The Palestinians say they own it because they were there first. The Jews say they owned it first. But if there are any Canaanites alive they could say they owned it first. They are all wrong.

In the Pentateuch, God reminds everyone that the land is HIS and He will give it to whomever He wants. In His unquestionable sovereignty, God gave it to the descendants of Abraham, Isaac, Jacob, and the twelve tribes of Israel. That is why the land belongs to Israel. Their parents' generation witnessed God's miraculous deliverance from their bondage in Egypt through ten plagues, fire, darkness, and the parting of the Red Sea. Then they wandered through the desert for many years. The Lord never abandoned them.

When was the last time you recounted precisely how the Lord has blessed you? There is no time like the present. Take a moment to recall the signifi cant milestones that God has accomplished in your life.

**Like Joshua, write a short summary.**

When I did this exercise, I had to go back later and add to the list as I continued to recall God's blessings. So perhaps leave room at the end of the list because God is not done yet.

**Read and write out Joshua 24:13.**

One word comes to mind as we read Joshua's calm words: *peace*. Despite the hardships and struggles he faced, Joshua's serene departure points directly to the provision and peace of God.

What do the following verses tell us about God's peace?

**Colossians 3:15**

**John 14:27**

Even when we experience life's dark moments and our circumstances offer us no peace, by the grace of God we can let the peace of Christ rule in our hearts.

Joshua's summary comprised the entire conquest of God's salvation victory in the lives of His people. He pointed out how God handed them a ready-made land that included homes, roadways, farms, and crops. Once God drove out the Canaanites, the Israelites just walked in and set up shop.

God not only marched with Israel's armies but He went before them to pave the way for victory. God does the same with you and me. Through Christ's perfect sacrifice and glorious resurrection, God conquered our powerful enemies of death, sin, and the devil. No matter what battles we face, God marches with us and goes before us.

## GO QUIET, GO DEEP

Quiet your mind from distractions and pull your Bible close. Bow your head and ask Jesus to make His Word and today's text personal for you.

Take your time writing out 2 Timothy 4:7–8.

What does it mean to you to fight the good fight and finish your Christian race well?

I pray that by the time the Lord calls you home, your life stands as a beautiful ebenezer of praise to the Lord.

## Day 3

# Choose Whom You Will Serve

*(Joshua 24:14–28)*

It is convicting when our words are put to the test. If we have not walked the walk, then our talk is hollow. If your life as a believer is not a model of Christlike living, it is never too late to start. If you are still breathing, there is still time.

*Serve* is a keyword through Joshua 24:14–18. In fact, "serve" appears more than a dozen times (depending on which translation you use). Although the definition and context of each occurrence may alter slightly, the idea is the same: Who gets your unwavering loyalty? For whom do you work? To whom or what do you delegate your time, talents, and resources?

Joshua first appears in Scripture as "Moses' assistant" (Joshua 1:1), but when all is said and done, he is called the "servant of the LORD" (Joshua 24:29), the same as Moses. Being a servant of the Lord means being someone who worships the Lord and carries out His will.

**Read Joshua 24:14–15. What does Joshua tell the Israelites in Joshua 24:14?**

Joshua lists all of the works and mercies of God and tells the Israelites not only to serve the Lord but to fear Him. This portion of the book of Joshua looks like Romans 12. In the first part of the book of Romans, the apostle Paul lists the mercies of God and His great works.

**Then what does Paul say in Romans 12:1–2?**

When we experience God's soul-saving salvation and His wondrous works of grace and mercy, the result is transformation from the inside out.

**Write the last sentence of Joshua 24:15.**

Joshua not only called upon the nation to fear the Lord and serve Him faithfully, but he went so far as to offer himself and his household as role models. In other words, Joshua's talk matched his walk. And the Israelites knew it.

**Could you, like Joshua, offer up your life as a model of God-honoring living? Why or why not?**

**Are you as clear and unambiguous as Joshua in your commitment to the Lord? Whether in public or private, what situations do you tend to most often wrestle with faithfulness and steadfastness to the Lord?**

Take time to write out the following verses. Pick one or two to memorize to address your area of weakness.

**1 Peter 1:6–9**

**Ephesians 6:12–13**

**Romans 8:35–39**

We need to be clear: Joshua's words are not an invitation for the Israelites to follow other gods. Joshua is drawing a vivid comparison between God's faithful power and the powerless, offensive manmade wood and stone idols around them.

Even though these are Joshua's last words to God's people (his last sermon, so to speak), he leaves them with a challenge: "Serve the LORD." He does not give pats on the back for a job well done or repeat words of praise; he simply reminds them to serve the Lord as he did: ALL IN.

**Read Joshua 24:16–28. In verses 16–17, what is the people's immediate response to Joshua's challenge?**

**In verse 19, what is Joshua's response to their proclamation?**

**In verse 24, what do the Israelites proclaim again?**

**What does Joshua do in verses 25–26?**

Joshua does not make a new covenant between God and His people. He renews the covenant the Lord gave through Moses at Mount Sinai. It is meant to be a blessing for the Israelites. Renewing their covenant would accomplish three specific things:

> [The] renewed covenant will continue to serve as (1) a mirror for the Israelites so that they know their sin, receive atonement in the sacrifices instituted by God, and trust in God's gracious covenant first given to Abraham; (2) a sanctifying hedge to set Israel apart from all other nations by its righteous ordinances; and (3) a shadow or prefiguration that pictures and previews the new and better covenant of pure grace in Christ.[26]

**What does Joshua say to the people in verse 27?**

Joshua's closing remark in verse 27 suggests that they are not quite able to convince Joshua of their faithfulness to the Lord. Not because the Israelites are insincere but because Joshua understands their pattern of faithfulness followed by idol worship. He had seen it in Egypt and he had seen it in the desert in the form of a golden calf. He knows it is only a matter of time before they begin chasing the world's idols, so Joshua reminds them what would happen.

We get the sense that Joshua realizes they do not know or are not serious about what they are committing to. It's almost as if Joshua says, "You do not fully realize how holy God is. He will not turn a blind eye to sin and idolatry. There is a cost of serving God."

**As a believer who serves the Lord, what is your understanding of the holiness of God?**

The holiness of God refers to the unparalleled majesty of His incomparable being and His blameless, faultless, unblemished moral purity. We gain glimpses of His holiness in Isaiah 6:1–5 and Revelation 4:1–8.

Joshua drives home the gravity of serving and honoring God. Twice Joshua has heard that they will follow the Lord, and twice Joshua has reminded them of the weight of responsibility of their commitment to a holy God. The Israelites understood clearly what God expected of them as His chosen people. Again, Joshua erects a stone and writes statutes and rules to serve as tangible reminders of God's covenant with His people and what will happen to those who break it. Like the stones raised on the other side of the Jordan, these visible reminders help them remember who they are and whose they are. Almost like pictures of family members to remember spousal commitments. Like an American flag to remember our freedom came at a great price. Like a cross to remind us that our spiritual freedom came at the greatest price: Jesus' sacrifice and resurrection.

Joshua's written words here are the first words added to the Pentateuch (the Books of Moses) that will make up the rest of the Bible (the biblical canon) as we know it today. Prophets, disciples, and scribes would add the rest under the inspiration of the Holy Spirit. What we hold today is the totality of what God desires us to know about Him, what He did for us, and what He expects of us.

The Israelites did not have the strength to keep all of the Lord's commands, and neither do we. We cannot fully serve the Lord in our own strength. We cannot overcome the temptations of life in our own strength. It is God's strength alone that enables our faithful service to Him.

When I lead tours to the Holy Land, Greece, and Turkey, I see visible reminders of God, His work, His faithfulness, and the commitment of His people in the past. Stones that remind our generation and those who come after us that we serve a living God.

Even though Joshua was a military genius and gifted administrator, the key to Joshua's success was his unwavering devotion to the Lord. His example continues to be a model for godly leaders even today. True success means being wholly dependent on the Lord, not our self-worth, wealth, or military might.

May our love and service to the Lord be as unwavering as Joshua's.

## GO QUIET, GO DEEP

Quiet your mind from distractions and pull your Bible close. Bow your head and ask Jesus to make His Word and today's text personal for you.

Take your time writing out 1 Peter 4:10–11.

What does it mean to you to use the gifts the Lord has given you to faithfully serve Him?

I pray that every gift God has given you is leveraged to bring glory to His name through your life.

DAY 4

# JOSHUA'S DEATH AND BURIAL

*(Joshua 24:29–33)*

The life and ministry of Joshua has come to an end. Born as a slave in Egypt, God chose him to lead His people to freedom in the land God had promised to Abraham. Now it is time for Joshua to receive his heavenly inheritance.

**Read Joshua 24:29–30.**

At one hundred and ten years old, Joshua (like the apostle Paul) could say, "I have fought the good fight, I have finished the race, I have kept the faith" (2 Timothy 4:7).

**According to Joshua 24:30, where is Joshua buried?**

We learned through the course of this study that Joshua was from the tribe of Ephraim. Is it any wonder, after he had fought for the Lord for eighty years (and probably more counting his time in slavery in Egypt), that he simply wanted his bones to end up with family?

I told you earlier in this study how my dad had served in the Air Force and is buried at Houston National Cemetery. However, I left out one important detail. A husband or wife is allowed to be buried with his or her military spouse in our national cemeteries. Dad was buried nine feet underground. Consequently, when Mom passes away, she will be laid to rest directly above him at six feet underground. There is something about knowing where your bones will end up. Joseph wanted his to rest with family.

**Have you chosen where your bones will rest? If so, what comfort does that bring?**

Joshua had some pretty big sandals to fill when God chose him to step into Moses' position. Yet, he did an incredible job. He completed all that the Lord expected of him. God gave Joshua His presence, as He had given it to Moses (Joshua 1:5; 3:7) and exalted Joshua in the people's eyes (Joshua 3:7; 4:14). God was faithful to Joshua.

As you have seen throughout the book of Joshua, Joshua's words carried the authoritative weight of the Lord, just as Moses' words had. People listened to and obeyed Joshua just as they had listened to and obeyed Moses.

Joshua had seen God free His people from slavery and bondage using dramatic miracles never seen by mankind before or since. He had experienced more desert-living than anyone other than Caleb. He saw the blessing of following God and witnessed the holy judgment on those who did not. He saw Moses carry the tablets containing the handwriting of God. Joshua was privileged to see more miracles of God than any other believer who has ever lived.

Joshua understood what it meant to be in a covenant relationship with God, and he lived accordingly. From slave to free, from wanderer to inheritance, from Egypt to the Promised Land, Joshua never focused on what he did. He relentlessly focused on what God did.

**What has God done in your life?**

**Read Joshua 24:31–33. What do the elders know according to verse 31?**

What an incredible tribute to their leader! Not only did Joshua wholeheartedly serve the Lord throughout his lifetime, but God's people had faithfully served the Lord as well. None had gone astray (except Achan who had been overtaken by greed).

Because of the Lord's faithfulness and Joshua's extraordinary leadership, Israel experienced the culmination of the Lord's promise to Abraham. And the elders reminisce that they had been a part of it. It is such a blessing for believers to remember our collective and individual histories with God.

One of the reasons that I lead tours through Germany in Martin Luther's footsteps and through Greece and Turkey in the footsteps of Paul is so we can remember what their faithful service to the Lord accomplished. By the grace of God, Luther was instrumental in translating the Bible into the language of the people and preaching the message of grace. Paul's service to the Lord resulted in Paul writing almost half of the New Testament that we hold in our hands today. Talk about inspiring!

Before we close our study of Joshua, I suggest a bit of further study as you have time. Grab your Bible and a notepad to compare the lives of Moses and Joshua. The Israelites were freed from bondage under Moses but could not inherit the land because they did not qualify. There was still way too much of Egypt in them. The Law could not bring them in because they could not earn God's favor. However, Joshua brought the children of Israel across the raging Jordan River into their inheritance.

The Promised Land was a gift of an unconditional covenant (Genesis 12; Genesis 15). That gifting of land was an act of God's grace, a free gift of God, given to them under the leadership of Joshua (Yehoshua).

**What does John 1:16–18 tell us?**

Joshua received the torch and completed what Moses began but never contradicted what Moses did. He completed what the Law said.

**What does Matthew 5:17–18 tell us?**

Jesus accomplishes for us what Joshua accomplishes for the Israelites under God's holy leadership.

Part of this Christian life is taking time to pass on to others what God has done for you. So why didn't Joshua train up another leader to take his place? The obvious answer is that it was not God's plan. God ensured that Joshua fully benefited from being mentored by Moses. Joshua learned both the positive and negative of leading God's people. God specifically did not choose a man for Joshua to mentor in such a way. Joshua trusted the Lord's judgment and never challenged His holy reasoning. Again, we could learn so much from Joshua.

We cannot forget that the book of Joshua hints that all would not remain well for the Israelites. Many foreign peoples (and their idols) remained entrenched within Israel's borders (Joshua 13:13; 15:63; 16:10; 17:11–12). That "occupation" would rear its ugly head during the time of the judges.

**What does Judges 2:10 tell us?**

What a sad thing to read after all that God accomplished for His people! However, are you and I any different?

**How has your life resembled the backsliding Israelites at times?**

Scripture is silent as to why God did not designate a leader to succeed Joshua. The people's later decay is not the fault of Joshua or God but rather the people's own sinful, self-centered natures absent a visible godly leader. Are we as a nation any different today? Are families any different today? The absence of a godly leader results in spiritual waywardness.

As we close, here's the bottom line: God buries His workers, but His work goes on. The great cloud of witnesses that has gone before us spurs us on to continue carrying the torch. When Moses died, God had already prepared Joshua. When Elijah died, God had already prepared Elisha. When the apostle Paul died, God had already prepared Timothy. In each of these instances, those whom God buried had actively mentored those who would follow them.

**If you are in any godly leadership position, who are you actively mentoring?**

May we carry the torch of faith as high and honorably as Joshua.

## GO QUIET, GO DEEP

Quiet your mind from distractions and pull your Bible close. Bow your head and ask Jesus to make His Word and today's text personal for you.

Take your time writing out Titus 2:3–4.

What does it mean to you to mentor the next generation?

I pray that the incredible blessings and lessons that God has taught you will be faithfully passed on to the next generation.

## Day 5

# REMEMBERING THE LESSONS FROM THE BOOK OF JOSHUA

Congratulations! We have reached the final day of our study. I do not know about you, but when I finish a Bible study I experience both a sense of accomplishment and of being overwhelmed. You did it! But how much do you remember?

You just completed a verse-by-verse study of the entire book of Joshua. Well done! But before you close this book, let's take time to remember one significant thing from each of our eight lessons as key takeaways from the incredible life of Joshua.

In each lesson, there was probably at least one thing that you learned for the first time or one new insight that blessed you immeasurably. Skim through the five days in each lesson and write one or two things from each lesson that will continue to bless you as you serve the Lord right now in this season of your life.

**Lesson 1: The Commissioning of Joshua**

**Lesson 2: God Will Make a Way**

**Lesson 3: The Fall of Jericho**

**Lesson 4: The Cost of Broken Faith**

**Lesson 5: Faith to Stop the Sun and Conquer the Land**

**Lesson 6: Victory and Parceling Out the Promised Land**

**Lesson 7: Cities of Refuge and Israel's Inheritance**

**Lesson 8: Joshua Finishes Well**

**What is one overarching truth or spiritual insight that God has given you regarding Joshua's life and service?**

# EPILOGUE

An integral motif throughout the book of Joshua reveals that God is a promise-keeping God. He faithfully prepared Joshua for leadership and gave him victory.

God did not give His people just any land. He gave them the land that He specifically promised to Abraham and his descendants.

God promised that He would be with Joshua. We have seen the truth and fruit of that promise. God promises that He will be with us as well.

The enemy will continue to hatch schemes, form unholy alliances, and play dirty tricks on us. But by the grace of God, like Joshua, you and I have chosen this day whom we will serve: the living God, the King of kings, and the Lord of lords!

He is our wall-flattener, javelin-holder, and sun-stopper. *He is the Lord God Almighty.*

As we put our lives in His holy care and keeping, I pray that you believe:

God knows the when, the why, and the how.

He knows the right time, the right door, and the right opportunity.

Like Joshua, we can trust Him wholeheartedly.

No worries.

No fear.

For the glory of His name. Amen.

# REFERENCES


Cherry, Kendra, MSEd. "What Is the Fight-or-Flight Response?" Verywellmind.com. https://www.verywellmind.com/what-is-the-fight-or-flight-response-2795194#:~:text=Pale%20or%20flushed%20skin%3A%20During,legs%2C%20and%20arms%20is%20increased (accessed March 30, 2024).

*Concordia's Complete Bible Handbook, Second Edition*. Concordia Publishing House, 2013.

*Crossway ESV Bible Atlas*. Good News Publishers, 2010.

Eames, Christopher. "Uncovering the Bible's Buried Cities: Jericho." Armstrong Institute of Biblical Archaeology. January 24, 2020. https://armstronginstitute.org/309-uncovering-the-bibles-buried-cities-jericho (accessed July 25, 2024).

Eames, Christopher and Rachel Grellet. "Uncovering the Bible's Buried Cities: Hebron." Armstrong Institute of Biblical Archaeology. July 1, 2018. https://armstronginstitute.org/46-uncovering-the-bibles-buried-cities-hebron (accessed July 30, 2024).

*ESV Study Bible*. Wheaton: Good News Publishers, 2008.

Ewing, W. "Shittim (Abel-shittim)." BibleHub. https://bibleatlas.org/shittim.htm (accessed July 24, 2024).

Gangel, Kenneth. *Joshua*, Holman Old Testament Commentary. Edited by Max Anders. B&H Publishing Group, 2003. ProQuest Ebook Central, https://ebookcentral-proquest-com.theoref.idm.oclc.org/lib/dtl/detail.action?docID=673842 (accessed June 25, 2024).

Harstad, Adolph L. *Joshua*, Concordia Commentary. Concordia Publishing House, 2004.

Hirsch, Emil G. "Book of Joshua." *Jewish Encyclopedia*. https://www.jewishencyclopedia.com/articles/8907-joshua-book-of (accessed June 25, 2024).

Howard, David M. *Joshua: An Exegetical and Theological Exposition of Holy Scripture*. B&H Publishing Group, 1998. ProQuest Ebook Central, https://ebookcentral-proquest-com.theoref.idm.oclc.org/lib/dtl/detail.action?docID=673062 (accessed July 4, 2024).

Jewish Virtual Library. "The Ark of the Covenant." https://www.jewishvirtuallibrary.org/the-ark-of-the-convenant (accessed July 24, 2024).

JewishHistory.org. "Joshua." https://www.jewishhistory.org/joshua/ (accessed June 25, 2024).

Kesselman, Shlomo Chaim. "Joshua of the Bible." https://www.chabad.org/library/article_cdo/aid/111849/jewish/Joshua-of-the-Bible.htm (accessed June 25, 2024).

Latvus, Kari. *God, Anger and Ideology: The Anger of God in Joshua and Judges in Relation to Deuteronomy and the Priestly Writings*. Bloomsbury Publishing, 1998. ProQuest Ebook Central, https://ebookcentral-proquest-com.theoref.idm.oclc.org/lib/dtl/detail.action?docID=436666 (accessed June 25, 2024).

Lawrenz, John C. *Judges/Ruth*, People's Bible Commentary. Concordia Publishing House, 1999.

LeWine, Howard E., MD. "Understanding the Stress Response" (Harvard Health Publishing, April 3, 2024). https://www.health.harvard.edu/staying-healthy/understanding-the-stress-response (accessed November 14, 2024).

McCoy, Samuel. "Uncovering the Bible's Buried Cities: Ai." Armstrong Institute of Biblical Archaeology. November 10, 2022. https://armstronginstitute.org/769-uncovering-the-bibles-buried-cities-ai (accessed July 28, 2024).

Mishaan, Iris. "The Biblical Use of The Shofar." ProShofar.com. January 23, 2018. https://www.proshofar.com/religious-articles/Biblical%20Use%20of%20The%20Shofar%20Old%20Testament%20VS%20New%20Testament%20.html (accessed July 26, 2024).

*NIV Archaeological Study Bible*. Zondervan, 2005.

*NIV Cultural Backgrounds Study Bible*. Zondervan, 2016.

*NIV Study Bible*. Tyndale House Publishers, 2008.

Pawson, David. *Unlocking the Bible: A Unique Overview of the Whole Bible*. True Potential Publishing, 2007.

Snow, Donna. *Meant for Good: A Study of Joseph*. Concordia Publishing House, 2023.

*Thayer's Greek-English Lexicon of the New Testament*. Hendrickson Publishers, 2005.

*The American Heritage Dictionary*. Dell Publishing Group, 1994.

*The English-Greek Reverse Interlinear New Testament*, English Standard Version®. Crossway Books, 2006.

*The Lutheran Study Bible*. Concordia Publishing House, 2009.

*Thompson Chain Reference Bible: New International Version®*. B. B. Kirkbride Bible Co., 1990.

Vine, W. E., Merrill F. Unger, and William White Jr. *Vine's Complete Expository Dictionary of Old and New Testament Words*. Thomas Nelson Publishers, 1996.

Wiesel, Elie. "Joshua: Silent at the Tent Door." Biblical Archaeology Society Library. December 1998. https://library.biblicalarchaeology.org/article/joshua/?_gl=1*19iuxri*_gcl_au*Mjk0Mjk1MTY3LjE3MTkzNDUyOTM.*_ga*MTc3NTkzMjEyOC4xNzE5MzQ1Mjk0*_ga_7MSGCYKLB3*MTcxOTM0NTI5NC4xLjAuMTcxOTM0NTI5NC42MC4wLjE1Nzk0ODI5MDk (accessed June 25, 2024).

Wiesel, Elie. "Joshua in the Bible." Biblical Archaeology Review (website). February 13, 2024. https://www.biblicalarchaeology.org/daily/biblical-topics/hebrew-bible/joshua-in-the-bible/ (accessed June 25, 2024).

# ACKNOWLEDGMENTS

To Mom, Lisan, Monica, Toni, and all my wonderful family who lovingly understand those times that I shut myself away from the world to research and write. You get it, and I'm so thankful. You are my joy and my greatest blessings on earth. I love you so much!

To Pastors Wayne Graumann and Doug Dommer for your excellent preaching and teaching at Salem Lutheran Church for decades. You laid an excellent biblical foundation that God continues to nurture. Your mentorship, support, grace, and love (alongside Kathy and Delo) are cornerstones in my faith walk. I love you very much.

To my Artesian Ministries Board of Directors: Rev. Mike Mattil, Rev. John Heckmann, Rev. David Bass, Sheri Jarratt, Belinda Burmeister, Heather Barratt, and Edith Walton. Your prayers, support, love, friendship, and wise counsel enable me to do what I love with excellence for the Lord. I could not do this ministry to the church without you.

To Pastors Tim Niekerk, Jason Schleicher, and Vince Parks, who continue to support me with prayer, encouragement, and biblical teaching even when my vocation calls me away from Salem on many weekends. Your friendships and counsel are priceless to me.

To the dream team at Concordia Publishing House: Jonathan Schultz, Elizabeth Pittman, Erica Sontag, Peggy Kuethe, Laura Lane, and so many others. Your hard work and commitment to excellence inspire me to be a better writer and student of the Word. I am blessed beyond measure to work with you and call you friends.

To my sisters in Christ in Salem's LWML group and daytime Bible study group. Your love for the Word and each other make me a better Christ-follower. Thank you for letting me bounce endless ideas off of you to bless others through this work. I treasure you, your continued prayers, and our friendships.

Finally, to Jesus. You know my heart, my desires, and my passion to serve You with every breath in my body. You know the good, bad, and ugly in my life, and You still entrust me with this ministry in service to Your church on earth. Thank You for giving me an undistracted devotion to You. I love You.

# ENDNOTES

1 Harstad, *Joshua*, 94.
2 Harstad, *Joshua*, 143.
3 *Concordia's Complete Bible Handbook, Second Edition*, 470–71.
4 "Winston Churchill's Inspiring Wartime Speeches in Parliament," BBC (website), May 8, 2020, https://www.bbc.com/news/uk-politics-52588148 (accessed July 24, 2024).
5 Harstad, *Joshua*, 175.
6 Harstad, *Joshua*, 203–4.
7 Harstad, *Joshua*, 224.
8 Donna Pyle, *Perseverance: Praying Through Life's Challenges: A Nehemiah Battle Plan* (Concordia Publishing House, 2019), 3.
9 Harstad, *Joshua*, 256–57.
10 Harstad, *Joshua*, 287.
11 *TLSB*, 352, fn 7:25.
12 *TLSB*, 353, fn 8:1–29.
13 Harstad, *Joshua*, 348.
14 Harstad, *Joshua*, 361.
15 Harstad, *Joshua*, 384.
16 *TLSB*, 356, fn 10:12–13, as quoted from *Luther's Works*, American Edition, vol. 3, p. 289.
17 W. E. Vine et al., "Sword," Vine's Complete Expository Dictionary of Old and New Testament Words (Thomas Nelson Publishers, 1996), 253–54.
18 *NIV Archaeological Study Bible*, 322.
19 Harstad, *Joshua*, 539–40.
20 See Snow, *Meant for Good*, 13–14.
21 Harstad, *Joshua*, 618.
22 Harstad, *Joshua*, 632.
23 Levi Mendelson, "Cities of Refuge Demystified," Chabad-Lubavitch Media Center, https://www.chabad.org/parshah/article_cdo/aid/2684913/jewish/Cities-of-Refuge-Demystified.htm (accessed November 11, 2024).
24 Harstad, *Joshua*, 686.
25 Harstad, *Joshua*, 772–73.
26 *TLSB*, 379, fn 24:25.